Eugenie &
Kevin!

Enjoy!

DK

Praise for *How to Be Married (to Melissa)*

"Dustin Nickerson is a lot like me. Young, handsome, a former youth pastor from the Pacific Northwest, a comedian, and married to a woman out of his league named Melissa. The only difference between us is I'm Black, and he loves flannels. His book is a great guide on how to be married with his signature comedic touch. He's one of the funniest comedians I know and a dear friend. Like me, his marriage and family come before success. This book is going to make you laugh, think, and be a better partner. I can't wait for you to read it and I hope you enjoy it as much as I did."

—KevOnStage, comedian, podcaster, and producer

"Marriage sure is a puzzle. It's so hard and there are so many ups and downs, twists and turns as life kicks you in the teeth. It's also joyful and wonderful! Dustin, with darling Melissa, gives us a front-row peek into their very normal, hilarious, wait-are-they-spying-on-me-and-my-husband-relationship. It's insightful, helpful, and entertaining and as a comedian, I gotta have fun while I'm learning."

—Leanne Morgan, comedian

"I learned two important things in this book: the argument is almost never about what you're arguing over, and Dustin is as hilarious on the page as he is on the mic. Dustin and Melissa share their marriage and arguments with such vulnerability that I felt like a nosey neighbor, listening in and then turning to my husband saying, "Thank God we don't fight like that," right before we begin an argument about how we do in fact fight like that. I felt seen to say the least. If you want some relationship advice and to laugh a lot, this book is for you."

—Anjelah Johnson-Reyes, actress, comedian, podcaster, and author

How to Be Married

(to Melissa)

A Hilarious Guide to a Happier, One-of-a-Kind Marriage

Dustin Nickerson

NELSON
BOOKS

An Imprint of Thomas Nelson

How to Be Married (to Melissa)

© 2022 by Dustin Nickerson

Published in Nashville, Tennessee, by Nelson Books, an imprint of Thomas Nelson. Nelson Books and Thomas Nelson are registered trademarks of HarperCollins Christian Publishing, Inc.

Author is represented by The Christopher Ferebee Agency, www.christopherferebee.com.

Thomas Nelson titles may be purchased in bulk for educational, business, fund-raising, or sales promotional use. For information, please email SpecialMarkets@ThomasNelson.com.

Any internet addresses, phone numbers, or company or product information printed in this book are offered as a resource and are not intended in any way to be or to imply an endorsement by Thomas Nelson, nor does Thomas Nelson vouch for the existence, content, or services of these sites, phone numbers, companies, or products beyond the life of this book.

Library of Congress Cataloging-in-Publication Data

Names: Nickerson, Dustin, 1984- author.
Title: How to be married (to Melissa): a hilarious guide to a happier, one-of-a-kind marriage / Dustin Nickerson.
Description: Nashville, Tennessee: Thomas Nelson, [2022] | Summary: "Popular standup comedian and podcaster Dustin Nickerson delivers a hilarious and practical take on navigating marriage based on his everyday experiences as a husband, father, and an Average Joe who is still trying to figure it all out"-- Provided by publisher.
Identifiers: LCCN 2022003379 (print) | LCCN 2022003380 (ebook) | ISBN 9781400231614 (hc) | ISBN 9781400231621 (ebook)
Subjects: LCSH: Marriage--Humor. | Christian life--Humor. | Marriage--Religious aspects--Christianity--Humor.
Classification: LCC PN6231.M3 N53 2022 (print) | LCC PN6231.M3 (ebook) | DDC 306.8102/07--dc23/eng/20220304
LC record available at https://lccn.loc.gov/2022003379
LC ebook record available at https://lccn.loc.gov/2022003380

Printed in the United States of America

22 23 24 25 26 LSC 10 9 8 7 6 5 4 3 2 1

To, who else, Melissa Nickerson:
my moonlight, CFO, and RBA.

Contents

CONTENTS

Foreword

I have known Dustin Nickerson for roughly a decade now. He is one of the kindest, funniest, most hardworking people that I know. He makes me feel lazy and incomplete as a human being in the best possible way. But the most valuable friendships are the ones that make you desperately want to be a better person and Dustin is absolutely that friend for me. Most importantly, though, over these last ten years Dustin has singlehandedly renewed my faith in men. He likes to joke that nobody hits on him after shows. This is wildly untrue. I have seen it happen many times and it used to make me very upset. I'd think, *How can these women attempt to corrupt a man who talks so often about his wife and children onstage?! If you want a comedian willing to cheat, it's not that hard to find, ladies! Leave my happily married friend alone!*

It took me a few years but now I understand why. Women want to be with someone like Dustin Nickerson. Someone who is both a wonderful husband and exceptional father. Someone who will get onstage every single night and tell thousands of people how amazing his wife is. Dustin has told me many times that if Melissa were ever to die, he would "just become Robin Williams' character in *Good Will Hunting*."

He and I have spent a lot of time traveling together—countless early morning flights and long car rides—and I am always so grateful to be on the road with someone who not only is faithful and loyal to his partner but talks about her in such a consistently lovely way. (Some of my favorite Melissa compliments are "endlessly interesting" and "strikingly beautiful.")

Stand-up comedians are generally very narcissistic. Sacrifice is not something that comes to us naturally. But Dustin's marriage and family always come before his career, before his own comfort, before his own ego. His priorities are never out of order. I have watched him take the first flight out Sunday morning after Saturday night late shows—often on three or four hours of sleep—to make it home in time for a baseball game or just trampoline time. It is hard to say who I am most jealous of in the Nickerson family—Dustin for being married to Melissa, or their children for being lucky enough to grow up with Dustin and Melissa as parents.

This book will resonate with so many people, but it will also probably make you a little angry because who actually meets their soulmate in high school? Couples that have only ever been with each other are few and far between, but even with his rare, impossibly romantic story, Dustin manages to be blunt, realistic, and hilariously honest about how much work it takes to have a successful relationship. He and Melissa did not just get lucky and stumble into a happy marriage, they have worked hard to build one together. As someone who has gone to Dustin many times for advice about love and life, I am excited that others will be able to benefit from the wisdom I have personally received from him by reading this book.

(PS In the interest of total transparency, I have not read the sex portion of Dustin's book because he is basically my big brother and—*ew*. But I'm sure that chapter is great too.)

—Taylor Tomlinson

Introduction

Naked and Afraid

Not one time in my life have I read the intro to a book, so honestly, I'm impressed you're here. I don't like that pages haven't started counting yet. Roman numerals? Little *iii*'s? What's that about? You mean I'm reading but it doesn't count toward my total? I'm out. I know a scam when I see one.

With that in mind, I'll try to make this a good intro.

I got married at the tender age of nineteen, which tells you right off the bat that I've made some questionable decisions. Melissa was twenty at the time and chose to marry *me*, which shows she might have even worse judgment. Yes, we got married before we could drink (legally, that is—thanks again for the bottle of champagne, Aunt Darlene).

Like any marriage, my relationship with Melissa hasn't always been a picnic. (Though there have been fights over food, plenty of bugs, and someone not getting enough blanket, so maybe it has been a picnic, actually.) But over the last twenty years, we have figured out how *not* to get divorced. To us, that feels like an accomplishment.

INTRODUCTION

As soon as Melissa and I got engaged, the relationship book recommendations came pouring in. Some were written by pastors, others by psychologists, and others still by self-help gurus. Each one was filled with neat-and-tidy programs and principles, acronyms and aphorisms, systems and silver bullets. Who knew that making marriage work was as simple as following seven principles or that love operated according to four universal laws?

Captivated by the promises made on the books' covers, Melissa and I read a stack of them. One book would help couples like us "save your marriage before it starts." The author's pessimistic outlook—predicting that every relationship would end in failure if left to its own devices—felt bleak. Another book taught us to communicate using a list of love languages, which were limited to five that would suit every person in the world. Teenage Dustin was pretty bummed to discover that "sex" was not recognized as an official relational dialect. (Although wasn't "acts of service" sort of open to interpretation?)

Melissa and I still laugh at how unhelpful those books were. They were so useless, without exception, that they made us wonder if the friends who recommended them to us were actual humans in relationship with other actual humans.

The failure of modern marriage books is not due to poorly written content. They were written better than this one, I promise. Their failure didn't result from lack of information or research. They were better researched than mine. In fact, most of them referenced scientific studies and many of the programs had been tested in focus groups.

Their downfall is that they all began with a common assumption: all marriages are basically the same. The author would share a principle that improved *some* marriages, and the reader was just supposed to accept that this principle would improve *their* marriage too. It's a recipe for overpromising and underdelivering. And if there's one thing I know about, it's messing up recipes.

Let's just state the obvious: Whenever two people enter into a relationship, a one-of-a-kind creation emerges that has never existed and will never again exist. Each person brings a unique set of experiences and assumptions and beliefs and expectations and dreams with them into a marriage. They have a unique mix of emotional baggage that they may not even be fully conscious of. And in a marriage, unlike on Southwest Airlines, the bags do not fly free. They cost, at minimum, the money you spent on this book.

All of this creates a unique set of circumstances that will undoubtedly lead to (cue Liam Neeson's voice) a particular set of problems. Marriage books are written for the masses. They cannot possibly tailor their wisdom to every individual's needs and problems, which is why Melissa and I gave all the books away. (I would have burned them, but I've heard that's frowned upon and I'm bad at making fires anyways.)

A few years ago, I began to imagine a different kind of marriage book. One that was written for actual humans in relationship with other actual humans. A marriage book that recognized the one-of-a-kind nature of every marriage and refused to offer one-size-fits-all solutions destined to disappoint. And one that was willing to laugh at serious problems to take the edge off and lighten the mood.

This is kind of that book. I mean, it's trying to be that book for sure. But like I said, I was *imagining* it. So that book was way funnier, and on the cover it said "*New York Times* Bestseller" and I was skinnier with more hair.

I am not a marriage guru, and I don't play one on TV. (Although if you have a role open, let me know. I hear television pays better than comedy clubs). Instead, I'm writing this book as someone who, like you, is in a messy marriage with a unique mix of problems that need to be managed effectively if we hope to avoid an expensive first date with a divorce attorney.

Being married to another human, even for a long time, doesn't make me an expert in marriage. It makes me an expert only in being married to my spouse. I am the world's leading expert in how to be married to Melissa. I'm the only living human who has ever done it, and I've been doing it for half of my life. In this book, I've compiled the most hilarious and helpful wisdom I've learned from my experience. If it's not that funny or helpful, I'm sorry; it's the best I got. Besides, quit being so critical. You didn't write a book. (My apologies to all authors reading this.)

The discussion that follows taps into some of the most common reasons married couples get divorced. While some people need to divorce to establish physical safety or emotional well-being, because you're reading this book, I'm going to assume that you and your partner would like to stay married for the foreseeable future—and actually enjoy being in relationship too. That means we need to talk about difficult topics like finances, physical health, sex, and faith.

Since I'm a comedian, you can expect a lot of jokes about each of these things. I know, I know. Your therapist told you that marriage was no laughing matter, but I beg to differ. When we laugh at the hard things, they become a little easier to bear. A lot of the stories and advice in this book will make you laugh—and also improve your marriage. The rest of it will also make you laugh but won't apply to your unique situation. Feel free to eat the fish and spit out the bones.

Before our big day, Melissa and I enrolled in premarital counseling through our church. Normally this would be performed by a pastor, but we requested to work with an older married couple we knew. Melissa and I came to adore Geno and Rhea. They were funny and insightful, didn't take themselves too seriously, and were clearly in love. Geno was retired from the Coast Guard and Rhea was a nurse.

Geno and Rhea had selected one of those marriage books to guide our sessions together. The book came with weekly assignments, which had the effect of making marriage feel like homework. Once a week for a couple of months, Melissa and I would show up at their house, book in hand, ready for a deep discussion related to our weekly assignments. Thank God, Geno and Rhea rarely stuck to the script. They knew marriage was more like music than math. So this wise couple spent most of our time together sharing specific stories from their marriage. Geno and Rhea told us about their ugliest fights and how much they hurt. They shared areas of disagreement and how they'd navigated them. They asked us to consider which of their practices might work well for our relationship, and they gave us permission to toss the rest.

In twenty years Melissa and I have never referred to that (or any) marriage book we studied during our premarital counseling. But we've recalled Geno and Rhea's stories numerous times. For example, when Geno returned home after months of deployment, he and Rhea scattered coins all over their backyard and then asked their kids to retrieve them all. This created enough free time to, you know, do the thing you do when you've been separated a while. Melissa and I have never scattered literal coins across our property because, well, who has coins anymore? Not sure a debit card would do the trick. Yet whenever I return home from a comedy tour, we carve out time to be together—just like the principle we learned from Geno and Rhea.

INTRODUCTION

My hope is that this book will become your weekly sit-down with Geno and Rhea, or in this case, Dustin and Melissa. You won't find a lot of charts and graphs, but you will encounter tools to hopefully help you compile a unique set of practices that can work for you.

DUSTIN NICKERSON
Bean bag in my daughter's bedroom,
Winter 2020

Chapter 1

If You Like *Fight Club*, You'll Love Marriage

A couple of years ago, a *Huffington Post* lifestyle reporter asked readers to share the details of the fight that ended their marriage. An unfortunate man named Kyle said his seven-year marriage fizzled over a fight about lunch. A woman named Cherie recounted her eighteen-year marriage ending over a fight about her cell phone usage. And Matt's marriage crashed and burned when he called his children from a previous marriage "my girls."[1]

I think as an unmarried person you read those stories and say, "Oh my, I can't believe a marriage ended over something so small and petty." But as a married person, we read that and go, "Yeah, I can see that." That's because we know the arguments themselves are never the issue. They're always a symptom of the deeper problem.

In the twenty years that we've been together, Melissa and I have survived an estimated 82,396 spats. If current trends persist, that

HOW TO BE MARRIED (TO MELISSA)

number should increase by at least a thousand by the time of this book's publication. (Yes, that's correct. Writing a marriage book has *increased* the number of marital fights in my home.) While every fight in our home is different, they are always about something very, *very* important.

And I know for a fact it's not just us. To this day, I've never met a couple who didn't have at least one board-game fight. I've also never met a couple whose wounds from their board-game fights ever fully healed.

Yes, I've heard horror stories of games of Settlers of Catan that led to husbands settling on the couch. Games of Monopoly that left wives morally bankrupt. And games of Life that almost ended an actual life.

Melissa and I's board-game brawl was during a game of Scattergories in 2004, and it's been a point of tension for almost eighteen years. I promise you, she is seething right now realizing that this is being published without her getting to tell her side of the story.

If you're not familiar with this game, it's simple. Someone says a category, and you list something in that category that starts with the assigned letter. So if the category is Colors and the letter is *B*, you write down "blue" and the judge gives you a point. Simple. Fun. Anyone can win. The perfect setting for a verbal brawl that will be remembered for decades.

So here we are, playing a wholesome game of Scattergories with some friends and family. We are in the first home we lived in together, drinking hot chocolate, and laughs are abounding. It's the scene of a modern-day Rockwell. The only problem is that as the game is winding down to its last round, Melissa and I are tied for first place. Whoever gets the next point wins the game.

The category: Things in the Ocean.

The letter: *W.*

The timer starts.

Melissa immediately buckles under the pressure and writes "whale." This is, of course, accurate but if any other player has the same answer, you don't get the point. There's no way someone else isn't gonna write "whale." A complete choke from Melissa.

I dig deep. I pass over my initial thought of "whale" and reach to the depths of the ocean itself as the buzzer sounds.

I write "water."

Because what, if not water, is in the ocean?

But I know I will need to do some convincing. This will not be accepted without heated debate.

Melissa reads "whale" and it gets canceled out immediately. There's no way that basic answer was making it through. She knows she blew it and that her only hope is to tear me down. She's in a desperate situation. It's honestly a little sad and pathetic. But she's no quitter, and I admire her tenacity.

I say, "Water."

The group is instantly divided. I knew it was going to come down to a vote. I make my case. Very articulately, I appeal to the judges (the other players) that the ocean is *not* water; nay, it *has* water. It is full of many things. The ocean is no more water than it is seaweed and fish. "Ocean" is simply the collective term for all the things that make up that which is the sea. I remind them the sky is not air; it *has* air.

The judges are persuaded. Water is in the ocean.

Melissa is furious. She rolls her eyes so far to the back of her head they touch her shoulder blades. I tell her, "There was a vote! If you're upset, you're not upset with me. You're upset with democracy." Melissa's anger is tearing down society—that's what I'm getting at.

Note for Melissa reading this at home: I know this isn't how you remember the story but (a) it's how I remember and (b) it's much funnier this way. They paid us a decent amount of money to write this book, so let me punch it up a bit.

Sometimes you have a fight so big it doesn't end the game; it ends the party. That's what this fight was. A game of Scattergories caused our friends to scatter from our home.

MELISSA'S POV

Dustin paints a lovely picture here, but you should know that earlier in the game, he'd convinced our friends to vote down my *A* word, *air*, by arguing that it was not found in the sky.

Why, oh why, did we put Scattergories on our wedding registry?!

- - - - - - - -

This is a prime example of a silly fight that was about something else. Of course we weren't fighting about the game and silly words. So what was it about, then?

For starters, we both hate to lose. We're prideful. We're competitive. Melissa has constantly been compared to her high-achieving siblings, and I constantly needed to be good at things to prove my self-worth. In our different ways, we both feel we lack value, and we project those insecurities onto each other.

Plus, winning is *way* more fun. Just ask me after the game of Scattergories.

But since that fateful day, we've grown. We've progressed as a couple and all our fights have been much more serious in subject matter ever since. Because Melissa and I would *never* fight about something silly again, right?

Hahahahahaha. Wrong.

In fact, just last week, we had a serious disagreement about an incredibly weighty matter, which went down like this:

Dustin: Being on the road is really taking a toll on me, you know? I'm exhausted from traversing the country like this.

Melissa: Traversing?

Dustin: Yeah, traversing. You know, like traveling, jet-setting, exploring.

Melissa: (*laughing*) Have you been reading a thesaurus behind my back?

Dustin: What's that supposed to mean?

Melissa: I've just never heard you use that word before, that's all.

Dustin: Is *traverse* the only word in that entire sentence that you managed to hear?

Melissa: No. But it struck me as odd. I mean, you managed to get a college diploma without ever taking the SAT. Are you still trying to prove something with vocabulary words?

I should pause here and point out that Melissa was making a factually true statement. Due to a procedural issue, I managed to get accepted to the University of Washington, an academically rigorous school, without taking the SAT. Melissa's dad once told me, a while after I graduated, that I should go back and take the SAT "just to see how you measure up." So I feel insecure whenever anyone brings it up.

MELISSA'S POV

Since Dustin is being so honest, I will share that my SAT score was the lowest of my siblings'. It's too bad the SAT doesn't take into account how many school dances and food drives you plan. Those dance themes and invitations didn't make themselves. What I lack in academic prowess, I make up for in my creative aesthetics of art and design. (Did you see me sneak those SAT words in there?)

- - - - - - - -

My SAT scores are one of my and Melissa's trip wires. You know, those issues and events that, if brought up, will immediately trigger all-out guerrilla warfare. Melissa and I have learned it's better for us to identify and even name our trip wires so we can do a better job avoiding them. This day, however, Melissa tripped my SAT wire, and I erupted like Mount Saint Helens.

I'll spare you all the gory details, but our fight turned out to be one for the books. A real dandy. It had everything a person could hope for in a marital spat—lots of action, tons of defensiveness, a handful of haymaker insults. I even told her I thought she'd inherited the worst traits of both of her parents, which went over about as well as you might imagine. In hindsight, we should've sold tickets to the neighbors. For more than an hour,

our kitchen was basically a *Rocky* sequel. Minus the presence of a muscular man, of course.

All of this because of a stupid vocabulary word. And Melissa wasn't even trying to start a fight. She just noticed something and commented. Looking back on that conversation, here's a breakdown translating our communication:

Dustin: Being on the road is really taking a toll on me, you know? I'm exhausted from traversing the country like this.

Translation: I am tired. The road is hard. Please empathize.

Melissa: Traversing?

Translation: Dustin has never said that word before, and it caught my attention.

Dustin: Yeah, traversing. You know, like traveling, jet-setting, exploring.

Translation: Does she not know what that word means?

Melissa: (*laughing*) Have you been reading a thesaurus behind my back?

Translation: Is he saying I'm stupid?

Dustin: What's that supposed to mean?

Translation: Is she saying I'm stupid?

Melissa: I've just never heard you use that word before, that's all.

Translation: I've just never heard you use that word before, that's all.

Dustin: Is *traverse* the only word in that entire sentence that you managed to hear?

Translation: Why don't you care about the way I'm feeling, and why do you think I'm stupid?

Melissa: No. But it struck me as odd. I mean, you managed to get a college diploma without taking the SAT. Are you still trying to prove something with vocabulary words?

Translation: You're projecting on me and I don't want any of that, so let me unravel you.

This is what I mean when I say that the fights are never about the fight themselves. Fights are the cracks in sidewalks caused by the roots from the tree in the yard.

Activity Time!

You're gonna fight—it happens. It's not an *if*, it's a *when* and *what about*. With that in mind, here are some low-stakes topics that, in my experience, are fairly safe to fight about. Remember when you were a kid and you'd play poker with the chips, but they didn't represent money? It's like that.

- Best episode of your favorite show
- Is ketchup on eggs a sin against God?
- Worst band of the '90s (there are no wrong answers, but "Limp Bizkit" is the right answer)
- Dumbest thing we studied too much in school
- More embarrassing footwear: Crocs or Heelys?
- Best Dorito flavor
- Of the family uncles, which one is the worst?

Happy fighting!

Planes, Trains, and Anger Mobiles

Melissa and I have learned that location makes a difference. Our fights may be private or public, by ourselves or in the presence of friends, sitting on the couch or standing on aisle 5 of the grocery store. But our worst fights happen when one of us is driving. I don't know what it is about sitting in a car that makes our claws come out, but we have had our best and biggest fights there. Our 2013 Honda Odyssey basically becomes the Roman Colosseum on wheels. Minus the presence of a muscular man, of course.

What is it about automobiles that brings out the boxing gloves?

I think it's because it takes a lot of energy to remain alert to other drivers while observing traffic signals so that you don't die before picking up your dry cleaning. Listen, I'm already grumpy if I have to both get dressed *and* leave the house. So if you add a traffic jam to the equation, even asking me a question is a hazard to your physical and emotional health. It doesn't help that I get carsick, and because of that, I do 100 percent of the driving (when I'm not puking) and insist on controlling the music with the tyranny of a less-than-benevolent dictator.

There's also the fact that while riding in a car, you're trapped. Cruising down the interstate at sixty-five miles per hour, you have nowhere to go. It's just you, your spouse whom you currently wish wasn't your spouse, and two lava-hot coffees between you. Have I ever been tempted to throw my coffee at Melissa? No, absolutely not. I'm not a monster. But have I ever hoped Melissa would sip her coffee, burn her tongue, and lose the ability to talk for an hour? I mean, technically no, but it was very easy for me to imagine that scenario right now, so draw your own conclusions.

It's a Family Tradition

I am pretty sure I inherited my championship car-boxing skills from my parents. They got divorced in 1990 when I was in kindergarten. That same year my grandpa died and my dog Murphy left. No, Murphy didn't run away. He left. He legit packed up his belongings and trotted down the street to another family's house and decided to live there instead. Basically, 1990 was the 2020 of my childhood.

I don't remember much about the years when my parents were married. But I do recall my dad's big blue Chevy conversion van. It had track lighting and a bed. A road trip dream. He nicknamed it the Enterprise, since he loved *Star Trek: The Next Generation*, and that was the only thing that made him feel like Jean-Luc Picard. In hindsight, the Enterprise was the perfect name for Dad's van because whenever we climbed inside of it, danger ensued and shields were raised.

One time my parents, my sister, and I had been seated in the car for less than a minute when an argument ensued. The insults bounced back and forth like a Ping-Pong ball. I have no idea of what was actually said. I just know they were mad and it was loud. As I look back on the story, as a current car fighter in my prime, I'm almost impressed. I mean, we hadn't even pulled out of the driveway yet.

Another time, a particularly nasty fight broke out when my father was driving the family down the highway. Having had her fill, Mom screamed at Dad to stop the van and let her out. He complied, and she flung open the door with the strength of a Klingon and started to step out. That's when I unbuckled my seat belt and declared, "I'm getting out too." (Man oh man, was I ever a mama's boy.) As I collected my belongings, Mom looked at me and then looked at Dad. She climbed back in, and we drove off in silence. Speaking as a parent today, I know that nothing is quite as sobering as one of my children having to become the only adult in the room. I'd love to say that's never happened to us. But I couldn't say it hasn't happened to us this week.

I don't judge my parents for these car fights. In fact, I've carried on their legacy. I'd like to say that once Melissa and I realized how I replicated my parents' unhealthy pattern, we worked with a licensed therapist to create a system to prevent car fights. But nope. We haven't done that. Melissa and I are the kind of couple who want to improve our marriage but sometimes resist doing the work and making necessary changes. (I'm sure you don't know any other couples like us.)

The Hazards of Mixing Exercise with Arguing

During the coronavirus pandemic it became clear that we should absolutely never have a fight while performing physical exercise of any kind. Soon after COVID-19 broke out, Melissa and I took up running together. Yep, things had gotten so bad that we were forced to resort to cardiovascular exercise. It was a tough time for all of us. But it turned out to be the perfect hobby for me during this terrible time because it helped me keep everything in perspective: No matter how uncertain life felt and no matter how bleak the news was, I could trust that running would always be the absolute worst part of the day.

But let me clarify. When I say that Melissa and I took up

running, I mean that *I* took up running. Before the pandemic, I would go on an occasional "run," which always started as a joke and then slowly devolved into a walk. On the other hand, Melissa has always been a prolific runner. And she's not the "take a selfie at the local 'Mimosas and Mojito 5K'" type of runner either. She's the kind of runner who does it until she sweats. When I met her, I had just quit all sports after my sophomore year in high school and was gaining weight like I was getting ready to be butchered. She was a high school track-and-field star who would go on to be a collegiate runner. (What were her personal records and placements in state? Please don't ask, because that's another trip wire.) But during the pandemic Melissa and I took up running together.

One particularly hot San Diego afternoon, we had a disagreement about finances. We were planning a charity event and disagreed over how much money should be allocated for a donation. Melissa handles our finances, so she tends to be more fiscally conservative. Since I am relationally insecure, I tend to use material gifts to gain others' approval.

Now here's the thing about being married to someone as long as I have been married to Melissa: whenever you're losing an argument, you can *always* weaponize history. If I feel backed into a corner or out of options, I reach for the past and club her with it. That day, as we rounded a turn and approached a fork in the road—both literally and metaphorically—I told Melissa she was "being cheap, like always." (You know it's a banger of a fight when you drop in an "always" like that.)

And that's when Melissa did her best Robert Frost impression and took the road less traveled. She took the fork in the road, turning down a less busy street than our normal route. Melissa was smart enough to realize that no one is obligated to dialogue with a person who is insulting them. She stepped away to calm down. Because she did, I was able to catch my breath too.

Melissa and I have learned that our marriage is best served when we are arguing about the right *what* in the right *where.* That means that going on a run when we're already angry is, um, ill-advised. It's just not wise for us to engage in a physical activity that increases our body temperature when our emotions are already hot. When we violate this rule, we've realized that taking a solo walk is a pretty good idea.

That day, Melissa beat me home by ten minutes. I entered the house and immediately apologized for calling her cheap. Now that our anger had had time to cool, we were able to talk and better understand where each of us was coming from. And that helped us move on.

Apologies and Acceptance

No matter where a fight erupts, or why, we believe it's critical that we end it in the right way. This usually means that someone—perhaps, ahem, me—needs to apologize for something. Contrary to popular belief among husbands, conceding a point is not the same as saying "I'm sorry." Sometimes I miscommunicate, crack a joke in poor taste, criticize Melissa's parenting decisions, or sit down for dinner and mutter, "Really? We're having chicken again?" The only solution to my comments is a heartfelt apology.

I've heard other marriage-guru types say you need to learn to "fight well." I disagree. You need to learn how to *end* the fight well. There are a lot of poor ways to end fights, and I'm pretty sure we've used all of them. Cheap shots and low blows, ultimatums, sarcasm, shutting down . . . I mean, these are all textbook Dustin-and-Melissa fight moves.

But every once in a while we like to break script and *not* end a fight poorly. We'll decide to take a minute to cool down, maybe remove ourselves from the situation to calm our chaotic emotions, and once in an especially blue moon, one of us might even try to understand where the other person is coming from. If you've ever seen one of us do this, it's essentially the same as spotting Bigfoot.

That's because ending fights is hard. You can be feeling so many things: anger, hurt, sadness, competitiveness, contempt, pride. And no matter what you're feeling, you're feeling it at 100 percent. There is no subtlety in emotions or feelings during fights.

Recently a friend told me that she and her boyfriend have a safe word that, when used, immediately ends the fight. I told her that's not what most couples use safe words for.

She responded that a therapist gave her the idea and it's been very helpful. Their word is *Pop-Tart*, and if either of them uses it, the other person has to respect their partner in that moment and stop arguing. The fight ends right there, no matter what.

This sounds like a great idea, but I'll tell you, it wouldn't work with Melissa and me. I have a bad memory and a bad temper. That means I'm going to forget the word and she's going to get mad at me for saying "papaya" out of nowhere.

Conceding can be a struggle for some people, and by some people, I mean me. Even though my first job as a teenager was at AMC Theatres and my job title was literally Concessionist, I'm still no good at it. Luckily, Melissa isn't either. She will be the first to tell you that she is not an apologizer. It's just not her thing. Never has been. She's lovely and kind and—except for the one time that she had too many IPAs and declared to the entire Red Robin parking lot in Salem, Oregon, that she was "incredibly talented"—humble. But she has a hard time apologizing.

MELISSA'S POV

It was two IPAs on our anniversary-slash-work trip. And yes, this character trait of mine is entirely true. I'm almost forty years old and still struggle to apologize. My preference is to just sweep conflict under the rug and move on, completely avoiding the elephant in the room. Who says avoidance isn't healthy?

- - - - - - - -

No matter which of us has caused the hurt, we find a way to set aside our pride, understand the other person's feelings, and eventually say we're sorry. Sometimes, however, the solution to a fight isn't an apology. It's acceptance. Melissa and I disagree about a lot of issues and ideas, and in many cases, no amount of arguing will fix that.

This became clear during a clash Melissa and I had in our kitchen soon after our second child, Gloria, was born. The location was a better setting than our minivan. It was still a tight space, but at least it had multiple exits and we weren't moving at breakneck speed. It was one of those spats where neither of us had any idea what we were fighting about anymore or how to make the other person feel better.

Exasperated, I asked Melissa to just tell me what I could do to fix the problem. She took a deep breath and I could see her genuinely trying to articulate how she thought and felt. After a minute, she calmly replied, "There is nothing you can do to make me feel better."

At that point, I could either continue our pointless battle or accept that we had reached an impasse. Melissa's response brought us back to reality: sometimes there isn't a solution. Life is hard, and we were feeling the pressures of it all. Once we accepted reality, the tension released.

I've decided that if I want to be married to Melissa, then we should try to recognize why we're fighting, become aware of the bad habits we adopted from our own parents, and resist the temptation to vent our anger in the wrong place or at the wrong time. And when I forget these best practices, I need to swallow my pride and either apologize for my behavior or accept the differences in our perspectives.

That being said, water is for sure *in* the ocean.

Chapter 2

A Full Heart Won't Fill an Empty Bank Account

There are two types of married couples:

1. Couples who fight about money
2. Liars

Everyone fights over money. It's too important not to fight over. And it's not the money itself couples fight over (unless maybe you have strong opinions on two-dollar bills or something)—it's what money represents. How much money you have and how you spend it often feels symbolic of something much deeper. Money stirs deep worries:

- Are we going to be okay?
- Can we provide for our loved ones?
- The neighbors know we're doing better than them, right?

Melissa and I have discovered that the financial philosophy a person is raised with is often the financial philosophy they bring to the marriage. And it's likely that your spouse will bring a different or even competing philosophy.

Poor-Adjacent Versus Rich-ish

Melissa and I had very different financial upbringings that can be summed up like this: the Hoglund (Melissa's maiden name) kids and the Nickerson kids both needed braces. Today, the adults in one of the families smiles at a cashier in a grocery store.

Were the Nickersons poor? No. It's not that simple. We were "poor-adjacent." Not impoverished exactly, but certainly in the vicinity. My older sister, Jessica (or Jesika, as she went by for one rebellious middle school year), and I didn't even realize that we lacked anything. As is often the case, families without money all tend to live in the same geographical areas. All the houses in our neighborhood felt the same. Our friends wore similar clothes and off-brand shoes bought at Kmart.

My hometown of Federal Way, Washington, had rich neighborhoods and poor neighborhoods—and there were separate elementary schools for each. Over at Olympic View Elementary, I qualified for free and reduced lunch with basically everyone else, which didn't really affect my meals anyway because my lunch plan was asking friends if I could borrow $1.50 every day. That was the exact amount I needed for my daily lunch of Skittles and a maple-bar donut.

Today, when Melissa is reminded that I had to ask people for money every day so I could purchase lunch, it makes her sad. It makes me feel sad too. Not because I was so poor, but rather that I was in better physical shape back when I was consuming a bag of Skittles and a donut *every single day*.

Melissa didn't grow up rich, though. She's an Air Force brat and her dad was an officer. So in all the different hometowns she's from, she grew up "rich-ish." Her family was secure. They were flirting with wealth. They had extra things. And not just CDs and stereos. They had a pool. Sure, they bought only used cars, but they also went on ski trips. (Nobody who grew up poor knows how to ski. It's basically golf, except with snow and hot chocolate.)

And as an Air Force family, a lot of the Hoglunds' basic needs were met (other than the need of having a friend for more than three and a half years). But Melissa's family also budgeted. They would search for sales and deals like my family stalked deer. But they didn't do this out of necessity. It's like when Brad Pitt wears a shirt from a thrift shop. You're not sure if he's being fiscally conservative or ironically hip. Simply put, Melissa's family didn't worry about money.

MELISSA'S POV

It's true that the Hoglund kids did not go without. But four kids is also expensive. My parents were hardworking and not flashy, so when we'd eat out after church, it was a "two Diet Cokes and four waters" kind of dining. (And the Diet Cokes were for the adults.)

- - - - - - - -

Though Melissa's family moved around a lot, their socioeconomic status didn't change much. Mine, on the other hand, did during junior high, when the socioeconomic stratospheres converged and both rich and poor kids met in the fluorescent lighting of Saghalie Middle School. These years can be rough for any prepubescent child, and this dynamic added a layer of insecurity about the financial state of one's family. This was the first time I realized my family might be, *gulp*, poor. Or at least poorish.

To hide their lack, people who are poor learn to employ all sorts of hacks. I remember hosting one sleepover and inviting one of the rich kids, Tony. It was all fun and games until Tony asked me, "Where are all the other bathrooms?" That's when I decided I would start going to their homes for sleepovers.

I even switched the way I dressed. I went from a skater kid to a prep. I turned in the baggy jeans with chain wallet (only God can judge me) for a pair of cargo khakis and a puffer vest. I may not have been rich, but Lord knows I didn't want people thinking I was poor. Nothing says "my family is doing pretty good" quite like a puka-shell necklace and a Gap sweater-vest.

Life with Uncle Butch

When my parents divorced when I was in kindergarten, Uncle Butch moved in with my dad, my sister, and me. Part of the reasoning was that we needed a warm body in the home while my dad was at work and my older sister, Jessica, and I were getting ready for school. Close your eyes, and whatever you picture in your head when you hear "Uncle Butch," that's him. Butch had one son, named Tater. I mean, technically his name was Jimmy, but we called him Tater.

My uncle Butch, God rest his soul, was six foot six and whatever the opposite of svelte is. I think of him like a 350-pound balding

Yoda. He spoke almost exclusively in proverbs and catchphrases. Except when he was drunk—then he got more incoherent and confusing. Essentially, alcohol would switch Butch from Yoda to Jar Jar Binks. But I'm one of those people who likes *all* the Star Wars movies, which means I found every version of Butch endearing in its own way. Despite his flaws I loved him, he loved us, and he was a pivotal shaping force of my childhood.

That said, if I were to describe Butch's technique for supervising my sister and me, it would have been no more than "warm body in the house." We weren't neglected in any way. He just wasn't super hands-on. What I'm saying is, we knew Butch was always there. Wait—is Butch like God in this analogy?

But some days in the summer, when Butch was home after working a swing shift, we would wake up around 11:00 a.m. and binge daytime television. There were talk shows and soap operas, but the crown jewel of daytime programming was *The Price Is Right*. Little did I know that Butch was providing me with the only domestic training I was ever going to get. For years I could estimate the cost of most washer-dryer sets.

On one of these mornings, Butch, Bob Barker, and I had the joy of watching a contestant hit it big. Every step of the way, it was huge winnings. The kitchen set, the new car, they spun the one dollar, and then they topped it off in the finale with a vacation to Madrid. Pure dominance. Like nothing I'd ever seen. I think this was the first person the show actually lost money on—kinda like when Butch went to a casino buffet.

Butch and I were watching it like game seven of a World Series (something that, as a Seattle Mariners fan, I know about only hypothetically). I think we cheered louder than she did when she punched her ticket to Spain. As we both caught our breath, Butch offered me financial advice that stuck with me into adulthood. In his Johnny Cash baritone, Butch said, "You know what, Dusty? Money won't make you happy, but it won't make you sad." (Note: Butch is the only one who was ever allowed to call me Dusty. You may not.)

And in this statement, Butch perfectly encapsulated the Nickersons' philosophy of money: We don't have much. We know it won't fix all our problems. But hey, a little more would sure be nice.

I'll Take the Mo' Problems If It Means Mo' Money

Fast-forward to when Melissa and I got married. I was working, and she was too. We had a little money, but we didn't really spend much either. Our love was forged over hot chocolate dates and rummaging through thrift stores. This matured over time into black coffee and thrift store shopping in nicer neighborhoods. Word to the wise: rich people donate nice stuff. As the saying goes, one man's trash is another young married couple's blender for the next decade.

Thrift store shopping is one of the best hobbies a married couple can take up. Hear me out. It's basically a scavenger hunt with exceptionally low stakes, and it's easy to celebrate wins. If you haven't done it, I understand your reservations. Maybe you don't think there are any redeeming treasures to be found in a warehouse that smells like a wrestling meet. But let me tell you from experience, it takes only one barely used four-dollar Garfield Christmas sweater to change your mind.

But the best part is you'll almost always end up sharing sentimental life stories you wouldn't discover otherwise. A bright orange

Oxford T-shirt will remind you of a trip to Universal Studios. A weathered Russell Wilson jersey will remind you of your dad. An irreplaceable vintage Batman coffee mug that you'll use every day for eight years that your toddler will then shatter as they run away from their older sibling, who's chasing them with a guitar. Ah, memories.

But there's a downside to thrift shopping. It's the kind of thing that you can get away with when you're younger. But if someone sees you thrift shopping in midlife, they get worried. A sixteen-year-old shoveling through the bargain bin at "Next to New" or "Second Chances" seems eccentric but resourceful. A thirty-eight-year-old doing the same thing screams, "Help! I just lost my job." You can get added to a prayer list if someone from church spots you at Goodwill.

You know how I figured that out? Because I realized my emotions regarding money were primarily governed by what other people think. I don't need them to think that I'm rich, but I can't have them think I'm struggling. Who cares if I'm actually doing well as long as people *think* I'm doing well?

For lack of a better term, I call this my *money motivation*. My primary feeling when it comes to money. The thing that determines why I earn, spend, and save. So I manipulate the narrative. I present information the way I want to so people see me the way I want them to see me. Control issues? Never heard of 'em.

Getting Upgraded

I'm currently writing this while on a flight back home to San Diego from Nashville. I've been on the road for nine days, which is exceptionally long even for me. The airline upgraded me to first class because apparently God doesn't completely hate me, and I'm not drinking the free wine out of solidarity with my wife who has been managing our home and the kids for nine days without me.

First class is an intersection of struggle for my money motivation. I'm up here only because I got the free upgrade. I can't afford to sit here. I just travel a lot. Airlines are basically incentivizing absentee parenting, which is troublesome and also something for which I'm currently grateful.

The first time I was upgraded like this, I was nervously looking at the other passengers like they were going to discover I was a first-class fraud. I thought they were going to smell the poor on me. *Was I supposed to wear a blazer? Should I be reading the* Wall Street Journal? *Why don't I have a monogrammed luggage tag?*

What I've since learned is that it's not about money up here. It's not about luxury or comfort either. It's about one thing and one thing only: *power*. That's why they let you board first and place a free cocktail in your hand. It's so you can sit there half-tipsy and judge that parade of peasants who remind you how powerful you've become. Once the peasants have completed their shameful strut, the flight attendant casually walks to the back of the first-class cabin and shuts the privacy curtain just to drive the point home. Then they give you another cocktail and offer you access to the captain's bathroom. Real power stuff.

Over time I've become addicted to feeling this power on a flight. If I can't get a first-class upgrade, I reserve a window seat. That's the second most powerful position on a plane. You realize it at takeoff when you catch your seatmate looking out the window.

"Oh, you're enjoying the view?"

(Slams shade shut with a sense of unchallengeable authority.)

"Not anymore you're not."

Fifteen minutes later . . .

"Oh, you're taking a nap? I have to pee again. *Everybody up! I'm the captain of this row!*"

Our Several-Hundred-Thousand-Dollar Mistake

Melissa's money motivation comes from her desire for security. *Is it going to be okay? Are we going to have enough, or could we run out?*

She (understandably) wants to feel safe and secure knowing that our bills will be paid and our needs will be met. This means she has zero flash to her spending, and it's difficult for her to spend money on herself. It also means she's naturally more stressed and worried about money, no matter how much of it we have at any moment in time.

In 2007, these two vastly different money motivations came to a head. More specifically, they came to a house. More specifically, they came to a three-bedroom, two-and-a-half-bathroom town house in Lynnwood, Washington.

Melissa and I had joined the kind of church where members got married, had lots of kids, and purchased homes. It was a modern-day *Leave It to Beaver* theology, a vision for "family" that was literally preached from the pulpit. You know how Jesus was essentially homeless and Paul made tents? We obeyed by investing in property, just as the Lord commanded. And by becoming pregnant with our first child.

I became a youth pastor at the church, while Melissa was working as a graphic designer for a theater company. The year was 2007. We were freshly out of college, twenty-one years old, and pregnant! Together we earned about $60,000 a year, so we were a bit mystified when the lady at the lending office congratulated us on being preapproved for a $400,000 loan to purchase a two-story town house with a yard and a garage. And we didn't know the housing market was about to murder the economy.

Hooray! You are allowed to owe people a mountain of money— even though you don't have any!

Such were the times. In those days, if you wanted a house, you immediately got a house. Everyone who walked into a loan office was basically Veruca Salt. (The Willy Wonka character, not the '90s rock band, but I love you if you thought that's what I was referring to.)

The process went fast. There were multiple offers on the town house we'd chosen and several that were higher than ours. But the little old lady who was selling decided to give it to us because she was thrilled that "a young Christian couple" was going to buy it. In hindsight, it might have been better if we'd been atheists.

Melissa and I were college students when we got married. She was a junior at Seattle Pacific University and I was at the University of Washington (well, I was enrolled there—my attendance was another story). We were full-time students who both worked part-time and had internships. We were busy and our marriage didn't come with a honeymoon period. But our house did. For a few blissful months we enjoyed the idyllic life of American homeowners. We had housewarming parties and dinner parties and cocktail parties (mocktails when *those* Christian friends came over). We hosted friends and families to watch sports events and grill steaks we could barely afford. I even built a patio deck with my dad. Those were our "little townhome on the prairie" months.

But then, shockingly, the payments started to take a toll. We weren't making enough money. Period. Our loan payments and HOA dues totaled about 80 percent of our monthly budget. We were in over our heads. If Kevin Durant were standing on my shoulders, he would have been underwater.

We tried to cut corners, of course. But as I've said, we're already thrifty. If you're already buying bread from the discount bread outlet, how much more can you trim?

After months of watching our money dwindle, we sought advice. Our accounts were falling and our stress was rising, so we met with a financial adviser. The man worked out of his home, which I assume he owned since he went to our church, and he was immediately shocked by two facts:

1. Someone was stupid enough to let us purchase a house.
2. Melissa had a budget spreadsheet.

"Most people I meet with who are in financial trouble don't have a budget," he remarked. "You guys are actually smart with your money. But buying this house was dumb."

We're blushing.

He was right, though. We had made a several-hundred-thousand-dollar mistake.

But the good news was that the market had been good, and we could always resell! Such were the times. We bought a house, and then whenever we wanted, we could sell it and get even more money. We will be fine.

Morgan Freeman Voice: "They would not be fine."

After meeting with the financial adviser, we decided it was time to sell "the little town house that could" because a lovely place like ours would sell in no time. We'd walk away with ten or twenty grand and go back to renting. No big deal. The unit next to ours had just sold for $20,000 more than we paid, and ours was bigger and more valuable because it was an end unit.

But this was the autumn of 2008. The market crashed the day after we listed the townhome for sale. We got exactly two viewings in the next six months. Melissa and I now had a toddler, and whenever he cried, I would nod and whisper, "I know. Me too." Melissa and I have mastered the art of not just making bad decisions but making them in the worst timing. It's a real skill. Some people can't multitask that well.

We were running out of money and options. We switched real-estate agents, but no luck. We tried to short sell, but no bites. I started googling "How to get on *The Price Is Right*." We met with the adviser again and he gave us our options, which had gotten bleaker. In the end we walked away from the house. Seriously. We just stopped paying our mortgage. We decided foreclosure was a great way to give it back to the bank. Simple!

Morgan Freeman Voice: "It was not that simple."

As it turns out, banks don't love when paying customers stop giving them money. I guess when they give you a loan they, like, fully expect you to pay it back? Wild. Also, banks aren't dumb. To retrieve their money they send your contact information to the friendliest, least pushy, most flexible financial managers they can find: bill collectors.

If you were raised in a family like Melissa's and did not marry a stand-up comedian, you may not know who these people are or what they do. Bill collectors are the type of people who make you okay with believing in the existence of hell.

They would call my cell, and if I didn't answer, they would call my personal work line. If I didn't answer that, they would email. If I didn't reply to that or the calls, they would start calling the front desk and ask my coworkers to try to reach me. Their tactics were tenacity and humiliation. They want to make you feel bad, like you've done something wrong. Keep in mind, this was a church they were calling. What am I supposed to do, tell the receptionist, "Hey, if the bill collectors call, can you tell them I'm out helping people?" That sounds better than what I was actually doing, which was planning youth group games so dangerous they're probably illegal now.

For the better part of that year I received three to four calls a day. I get it—they were just doing their jobs. But I already knew I'd done something wrong. There was nothing I could do to fix it. We had no other option. So I would answer these calls and receive a beating multiple times a week. This was my penance, I suppose—that and filing for bankruptcy. Debt repaid, if you ask me.

Oh, and did I mention we were pregnant again? Yep. In fact, that's the only clear indication we had sex at least one time during that period.

Couple's Question!

What's the hardest money decision you've ever made? Buying a house? Losing a house? Sending the kids to private school? Going on vacation instead of sending your kids to private school?

Did that decision draw you closer together or drive you further apart?

Those are hazy days to remember. We were forced to leave our home and find a new place before Gloria was born. Melissa was so worried nobody would let us rent because we were in money shambles, had terrible credit, and were moving into bankruptcy. But then a friend who owned a home agreed to rent it to us for $1,000 a month. I will never forget his email to me after I explained our situation: "Your money is always good here."

It had only two bedrooms, one of which was a converted carport, and it was located across the street from a cemetery, which felt like a metaphor at the time. We gratefully moved into the house the month Melissa was due. The day Gloria was born, the first person to call me was a bill collector.

The Rat Kings

Two months after we moved into our friend's rental home, we formally declared bankruptcy and felt relief. It was over. Did we have some judgmental family members who thought it was immoral to declare bankruptcy and not pay off debts? Of course. That's what Christian family members are for. But we felt like a weight had been lifted. We were out from under the house before it crushed us like it did the Wicked Witch of the East—even though Melissa did wear a lot of striped socks back then.

We weren't thriving all of a sudden. You know when people say stupid things like, "We weren't rich, but we were rich in spirit"? Yeah, well, we were neither. We were battered and beat-up and had real damage on us to because of misguided financial decisions.

Recently Dave Ramsey's company conducted a study of more than one thousand American adults and found that finances are the number one issue that couples fight about and the second leading cause of divorce (behind infidelity).[1]

This stat is not only another reason I'm shocked that I'm still married to Melissa. It's also a warning for married couples who want to stay married to take these issues seriously. As Melissa and I learned, money issues are debilitating because they connect to deeper insecurities and emotional triggers.

Our troubles didn't just keep Melissa from buying bread at the regular supermarket. It also stripped her of one thing she'd always been able to count on growing up: financial security. Suddenly she was worrying about things that had never before been a source of anxiety. And this was disorienting for her. My dismissive responses and everything-will-be-fines were a coping mechanism, but they often just added pressure.

We both felt a lot of shame. Melissa would work hard to gently navigate well-meaning questions from her girlfriends. And I was constantly in PR mode, trying to craft a true-ish narrative about our lives so people wouldn't think I was a failure husband or deadbeat dad. But in reality, we were broke. We went from a home with three bedrooms to a bank account with three digits. We were struggling and had massive decisions to make.

Thankfully, friends and family stepped in to help. Money, groceries, gas in our cars. A friend had a dream one night that he had a chest full of gold coins, and in the dream God was telling him to give us the coins from his chest. Because of this dream, for months he helped close the gap for us. (I was thankful I hadn't gone the atheist route after all!)

This is a reminder of the importance of surrounding yourself with good friends in your marriage. It may take a village to raise a child, but it takes a city to raise a marriage. I'm not sure if that analogy actually works, but the important thing is to not be isolated in your marriage. That's the big takeaway here. You get it. If you don't get it, go ask a friend what it means. And if you don't have a friend to ask, well, that's the point.

I started working a second job at a homeless shelter (we weren't living there yet, but I thought I'd just start making connections). I'd do an all-nighter on Thursday nights because I had Friday off from my regular job. This left me in less than tip-top shape for the weekend.

Still it was tight. I added barista to my jobs and worked at Starbucks two to three times a week. And even though Starbucks is one of the biggest companies in the world, for the frontline employees it's a nonprofit. The free pound of coffee a week was nice, but Verizon didn't accept it as payment.

We were in a bad place. Should Melissa go back to work? Should we move? Should one of us go back to school? All this culminated in a move to San Diego (which I get is not typically the move you do when money is bad). One of my best friends had planted a church there and offered us a way out. Between the salary he would pay me and raising some additional support, we could make progress. I would work for him for a year, pivot into the rec center (more later on why this was the best job in the world for me), and start doing open mics to build my dream career.

We rebuilt from the rubble. Which is something married couples who go the distance often have to do repeatedly. We started living the way we should have all along—manageable rent, modest living, steady jobs, and a side hustle. To pay off college debt, we saved money and rented to roommates for extra help, starting a tradition. Right now our roommate's name is Don, and he's the best roommate we've ever had. Sometimes he has a poor sense of boundaries, but he's a grill master and buys wings for Monday Night Football. We can count on him for childcare, and we love him. Oh yeah, he's also my dad.

Pros and Cons of Adult Roommates

PROS:

- Helps with rent
- Built-in childcare
- Teaches you how to have sex quietly (it's more helpful than you think)
- Shared chores (always a win when you are cleaning the toilet less)
- Helps with rent

CONS:

- *Why is there another adult living with us?!*

Choose wisely, friends.

Lessons from Old Rusty

The upshot of financial problems is that they force you to do things you never imagined doing. Humbling things. Character-building things. The kinds of things that make hysterical stories when you're no longer a youth pastor / rec center middle management / open micer and have become a moderately successful comedian and someone (who I assume has a drinking problem) agrees to publish your book. Let me tell you about one of those things.

HOW TO BE MARRIED (TO MELISSA)

For the seven years Melissa and I spent rebuilding our lives, we had a trusted companion I called Old Rusty. In those Old Rusty years we relied on that 2009 silver Dodge Caravan. It had been Melissa's brother's family car while they lived in Chicago. Then, when they moved overseas, they passed it on to us. I flew to Chicago and drove it back home to Seattle. This was the only road trip on which Old Rusty did not break down.

I remember looking up the resale value of Old Rusty on Kelley Blue Book. It said he was worth $300. That means when I loaded up my groceries at Costco, I had doubled the value of my vehicle. Even by old minivan standards, Old Rusty was pretty rough. The AC didn't work. The cloth above the driver sagged. It overheated constantly. And for a while, every time you got gas, Old Rusty would randomly die at the next stoplight. Our mechanic told us, "I don't think this car is worth enough for me to figure out why it does that."

Old Rusty functioned as our main family vehicle for years, but he became my primary vehicle when we acquired a new (used) van. Good news is, I didn't drive it much. I would drive him to my job at the rec center less than a mile away and to local comedy spots. Those were fine because it was night, which meant you didn't need AC and it wouldn't overheat.

But sometimes I was forced to take him on longer trips. One time I interviewed for a job in LA, and I made the whole drive shirtless with the windows down because I didn't want to sweat through my shirt. I got there, got out of my car shirtless, and put on my clean shirt with only one person seeing me unkempt and bare chested. That one person? The guy interviewing me. I didn't get the job, and I cussed at Old Rusty most of the drive home back to San Diego.

However, nothing was as humiliating as taking Old Rusty through a fast-food drive-thru. In his elder years, Old Rusty's driver's side window quit working. But to go through a drive-thru you need two things: a human being and a car with a functioning driver's side window. I only had one of those things. After placing my order by yelling over my shoulder through the driver's side back window, I wouldn't stop at the pickup window like a normal person. I'd drive right past it, befuddling the cashier, and then open my door and angle my arm out to shamefully grab my items. You lose all your dignity in that forty-five-degree turn. I remember thinking, *Don't judge me. I fly first class.*

One time I went to Starbucks, and as I reached back to grab my items, the barista asked me if I needed a receipt. My response: "Do I look like a guy who's tracking his money that closely? You think I'm taking receipts home to log them in QuickBooks? I shouldn't even be here right now. This is clearly a splurge purchase. Dave Ramsey would be so disappointed if he spotted me here."

Melissa and I held on to Old Rusty because we were wising up. And as the business (Dustin Nickerson Comedy, also known as the DNC) grew, Melissa only got savvier. If financial problems don't destroy a couple, they will definitely make the couple savvier. During the COVID-19 pandemic, my gigs were canceled so I essentially stopped earning money. That's when Melissa worked the government like a guru and we stayed afloat.

MELISSA'S POV

One thing that helped Dustin get on board with saving was the idea of us "winning" at money. If he told himself to resist X (spending impulse) so that we could save for Y, then he could focus (ADHD aside) on a win like "pack a lunch so we can save that money for hipster coffee and thrift shopping."

– – – – – – – –

Thrift-Store Dinosaurs

We lived very modestly. We used the airline points I earned to go on vacations—sometimes the vacation itself would be centered around my work—and every once in a while we'd get craft coffee because that's our actual splurge. Just the coffee though. We wouldn't buy anything else in that coffee shop. That's where the real rip-off happens. For example, our favorite local coffee shop recently tried to sell me on a sixty-dollar tote bag.

Cashier: It's artisan. It's handcrafted. It's high quality. Feel the lining. The lining makes it worth it.
Me: Is it lined with fifty-nine dollars? Because if so, then yes, that's worth it.

Find Your ODT

I get it. It's dumb to spend money on expensive coffee from Starbucks when you're broke. But it's our "one dumb thing," or ODT (an acronym I'm confidently acting like we've used before but really I just coined). Here's my guide to picking your ODT:

- The spouse has to agree.
- You have to enjoy it together.
- It can't involve the kids because, well, their whole lives are an ODT.
- It has to be small. Like, for example, your ODT can't be a three-bed, two-and-a-half-bath townhome in Lynnwood, Washington.
- It has to be something you know would rankle Dave Ramsey because that guy is loaded and shouldn't be judging you anyway.

The Christmas we moved into our $1,000-a-month carport, our three-year-old son, Joel, had a thing for dinosaurs. He loved them more than anything. (Don't judge him; he wasn't a Christian yet and didn't know that the devil planted those bones so we'd believe in evolution.)

We knew we couldn't afford to get Joel new toys, and even though he would get some new toys from the family, we wanted him to get something from us, too, right? His parents? So we headed to the thrift store. Usually we're excited when we go thrift shopping, but for some reason, I was ashamed. I didn't want to buy my kids used toys. Maybe it has something to do with the toy area of a thrift shop. It's absolute chaos. Miscellaneous bags of action figures, guitars with no strings, and board games with missing pieces.

But on this day, there in the middle of this chaos, was a bin. A bin that looked new and was full of fifteen to twenty nearly perfect dinosaurs. Complete with trees and rocks and a mat where you could make a scene. This wasn't just a toy. This was an activity. He could act out scenarios with dinosaurs. Use his imagination.

When we inspected the set, all the dinos were perfect except the T. rex. One of his little legs looked like a dog had taken a bite off it. So the T. rex couldn't stand, but amazingly that made him interesting to Joel, who gave him a backstory. And the T. rex gave Melissa and me a reminder that things would be okay. That we would find a way. That we were limping and couldn't stand up straight, but now we had a backstory and could hold each other up.

That dinosaur meant the world to me, and I wanted to keep it forever. As a reminder of where we came from. A token of the past. Hope for the future.

Melissa threw it away. She hates clutter. And sentiment. And those dinosaurs. And maybe me. But the memory is still sweet, and just like money, it doesn't make me happy, but it doesn't make me sad either.

Chapter 3

I'd Like to Order a Happy Marriage. But Hold the In-Laws.

All you need to know about in-laws is that whenever someone has a good relationship with them, it's presented as a surprise: "You know what? I *actually* like my mother-in-law." We speak about in-laws the way kids speak about vegetables. If you enjoy them, you're the weird one.

There's no way it couldn't be like this. New adults just become your family. No background, no childhood together, no memories. Just a new set of fully grown humans with personalities and opinions that you're now expected to merge with. Imagine getting a new job, meeting your coworkers, and then being forced to spend the holidays with them. If there were a two-weeks' notice for in-laws, everyone would turn it in after the first Christmas.

When it comes down to it, in-laws are just regular people. They have plans and agendas and dreams that they usually want other people to fit into. And no one meets another person's expectations exactly. Now that I'm thinking about this, I'm getting more excited for my kids to get married so I can have a whole new group of people I don't like and who do not like me.

That being said, I've done my best to make it work with the in-laws from day one. I was quite young when Melissa and I met, and I can't tell you why, but young Dustin was *very* traditional when it came to relationships. I mean, sure, my family was full of relationships that haven't worked out, but why I thought adding manners and properness would be the cure—I'm truly clueless. Maybe I thought that came with the religious territory. Because when I went in, I went fully in.

I also figured I'd have to charm/trick a father into letting me marry his daughter, so maybe some ol' fashioned chivalry and courtesy would do the trick. Now insert into my life Air Force Lt. Col. Dave Hoglund, also known as Melissa's dad. Dave is a driven, accomplished, highly intelligent, type-A male. He's also detail oriented, hyperfocused, and a marathon runner. Until I met him, I had only heard rumors of these kinds of people.

We are complete opposites. The only thing we have in common is a love for Melissa. We're not besties; we're not enemies. We exist together in the way I think a father-in-law and the-guy-who-does-a-lot-of-weird-things-with-his-daughter should. Personally, I have zero intention of being buddies with whoever marries my daughters.

Dave and I couldn't be much more different. Even down to how we relax. If I go on vacation, I'm an all-inclusive resort kind of guy. Dave? His idea of a family vacation is having everyone help him retile the kitchen. At times, we quite literally have a working relationship.

What we did have in common was being on the traditional side. I'm not talking, "Did you ask Melissa's dad if you could marry her?" Of course I did. That's traditional 101. Four years before that day ever came, I was in the church foyer ("narthex" if you've got Lutheran ties like her side does), asking her dad if I could ask her to go to *homecoming*. I mean, that's some royal-family living etiquette right there. And not shabby for a guy who was scooping popcorn at AMC at the time.

Melissa's dad, in the ultimate pro dad move, pleaded the Fifth on Melissa's behalf about homecoming. "Well, I'll ask her," he said. "But she's really busy." Brilliant. He both let me down easy, and he gave his firstborn daughter an easy out. Dave's a veteran.

Couple's Question!

Who's your *favorite* in-law? You shouldn't pick favorites with kids, but in-laws? Totally fine. A lot of time is focused on the in-laws we don't like, so here's a positive spin. Which one do you like the most?

Dustin's note to Melissa: my answer is your mom with a glass of Chardonnay in her.

MELISSA'S POV

Hands down your *sister*, Jessica. She holds our families together with her kindness and willingness to always help through heartache, tragedy, and celebrations.

- - - - - - - -

All this properness aside, when the day came to ask Dave if I could marry Melissa, that was a big step up, so I was petrified. I didn't like being alone with him in normal circumstances, so asking if I could spend my life with his firstborn child wasn't exactly water-cooler chitchat. "Hey Dave, how about this weather? Anyways, if Melissa isn't doing anything the next fiftyish years . . ."

I'll never understand dads who are super friendly with the guys who marry their daughters. One time Dave walked in while Melissa and I were making out in her room (sorry to our youth pastor, who is just now learning we didn't *literally* kiss dating goodbye). This is a room that he paid for and a human he had made and raised. And here this punk kid is kissing her in it? He cleared his throat to make his presence known. We stopped. Now that I'm thinking of it, I'm starting to see the brilliance in all the manual labor.

Fear and Loathing in Lancaster

Because of a job transfer, Dave moved from Tacoma, Washington, to Lancaster, California, while Melissa and her younger twin sisters, April and Sarah, stayed behind with their mother, Charlene, for Melissa's senior year. Since her brother, Jon, was in college, I felt this made me the de facto "man of the house." (We were a month into dating at the time, and I was already convincing myself that I should try to be the alpha in the house.) I spent a lot of that year going to Melissa's dance recitals and track meets, to her sisters' basketball games, and on plenty of shopping trips led by her mom.

While Dave and I are civil, I've always adored Charlene. Like me, she grew up as a latchkey kid, and I think she knew that about me long before I confessed it. Perhaps there was an energy she could just read, where she knew I longed for a home with a loving mother figure. Or perhaps it's because whenever I came over I was always hungry, and I was way more appreciative of the meals than her kids were, since they had come to expect this weird thing called a "nightly dinner." Either way, we were fans of each other. Then again, she may have just been nice because I brought her raspberry mochas.

MELISSA'S POV

You're charming, Dustin, and you brought a lot of levity during a hard transition. We welcomed your company.

— — — — — — — —

Charlene and my dad did have things in common though. Most notably, neither of them could remember the name of our local fabric store on the intersection of 320th and Pacific Highway in Federal Way, the center of a fine marketplace. Malls, Best Buys, Old Navy, seven Starbucks in three blocks—everything you could need. In the heart of this mecca was a home store aptly called Linens 'n Things. This simple and to-the-point name proved impossible for them to remember. Charlene referred to it as "Linens and Such," and Don swears to this day it's "Linens and Stuff." It still makes Melissa and me laugh.

My dad gets so many words wrong that at this point it's hard to tell if he's just trolling us. For seven years I worked at a church as a "pasture," and my sister was studying "psycho-logy." But more and more I think it's a true mishap because the number of medical words he gets wrong can be worrisome. His "M-I-R scans," the shots from the "epidemiologists," and perhaps most alarming, his swollen "prostrate."

The rest of the family joined Dave in Lancaster the day after Melissa graduated from high school. But Melissa only spent the summer there because she decided to go to Seattle Pacific University and remain in the Pacific Northwest. She had stayed for me. Game. Set. Match. Sorry, Dave.

We would visit Lancaster from time to time, which was frankly asking a lot. I try not to exaggerate or use hyperbole too much, as you can already tell, but I cannot emphasize this enough: Lancaster is the worst city in America. The first time we visited, it was 118 degrees, which I didn't even know was possible or legal. Or compatible with a belief in the existence of a merciful God. The next time it was below freezing in the winter—but with no snow or hills or mountains or magic. Just the cold and nothing to stop the wind except your chest.

Lancaster had no culture, no identity, no activities, and was three hours from an airport. It's the type of place where you get excited when the Black Angus Steakhouse coupons come in the mail. Yet since it's still in Southern California, it wasn't even that cheap to live there. But Dave had a job at the Air Force base, so I don't blame him for moving there. I blame the military for expecting anyone to move there. I'm sure there were warlike conditions with better accommodations than this.

On one of our trips to the third circle of hell (honestly, it's worse than Dante imagined), I decided it was time to pop the question about popping the question to Dave's daughter. Everyone knew it was coming, and it was really a formality. But again, formality was kinda my thing. We went to the place where all good love stories begin—Crazy Otto's Diner, home of the world's largest omelet.

Not for one second would I knock this place, because Crazy Otto's has everything you want in a greasy-spoon breakfast joint: waitresses who don't make eye contact or let your coffee get cold, a Guinness Book world record, and not a vegetable to be found. That morning, though, I was so nervous I couldn't have eaten the world's smallest omelet.

I actually panicked while ordering, which is uncharacteristic of me. I am a decisive orderer. I labor over a menu. I talk through options out loud, weigh pros and cons, do a cost-benefit analysis. If I could bring a whiteboard in to discuss it with the group, I would. When it's time to order, I know exactly what I want and I make few mistakes. I honestly can't think of a single order I regret.

Melissa is the complete opposite. When it's time to order, you'd think she'd never been in a restaurant before. And it's not like she's overwhelmed; it's like she's just excited to be there. Melissa sits in a booth, looking at a menu the way people on roller coasters look right before they take off. It's a nervous energy that ends with her saying the first thing she sees when it's her turn to order, and with me putting my face in my hands because I know she doesn't want that.

How could she be so haphazard with her food item? That's why we're there! Correction: that's why I'm there. I go out to restaurants to eat. Melissa goes to restaurants to go out. It's part of the reason we don't eat out often. She doesn't appreciate the food and I don't appreciate the hang. I can't get out of there soon enough. When they clear my plate, I hand them my credit card. What? Am I just going to keep sitting here in this dumb booth? In a setting where it's considered rude to be on my phone? It's a no from me, dog.

HOW TO BE MARRIED (TO MELISSA)

I am so apathetic about restaurants and food. I love a good vibe and getting out, but I could happily live off oatmeal and coffee from any hipster coffee shop. Amazing food is lost on me. For a friend's fortieth birthday, a group of us went to Mexico for wine tasting and a multiple-course, long-table, family-style dinner. Everyone *oohed* and *aahed* when each course arrived, and I thought the cucumber agua fresca I kept getting refilled was the belle of the ball.

Strawberry-Pancake Proposal

Thankfully for me, this trip to Crazy Otto's was gonna be short. Neither of us really wanted to be there. I had good intentions and was a fairly safe bet as far as sons-in-law go. Dave knew that the most important thing was that I loved Melissa and she loved me. We were young and in love, but we weren't haphazard. The foundation for a strong, lasting marriage was there.

That's not to say Dave was excited. The bottom line was, I was essentially asking Dave if he could pay ten grand for a preparty to celebrate that I was going to take his daughter's virginity. I had zero idea how this whole event was gonna go. It was my first time. It was Dave's first time. It was likely Crazy Otto's first time.

I was nervous and off my game. Like I said, I was so uneasy that I even messed up my food order. Yes, the unthinkable happened. Mr. Decisive Food Orderer missed the mark. I was so focused on those first words, how to get into the topic, that I wasn't thinking about the menu.

My brain was trying to come up with answers to the standard questions—answers that were better than my honest thoughts:

Dave: What do you want to do with your life?
Me: Undecided.
Dave: How are you gonna provide for my daughter?
Me: Unknown.
Dave: How many kids do you want to have?
Me: Uninterested.
Dave: Are you invested in the stock market?
Me: Unable.

(Cue waitress)

Waitress: What can I get you fellas?
Dave: Strawberry pancakes.
Me: Uhhh, I'll have the same.

What. Are. You. Doing. Nickerson?
I've never ordered strawberry pancakes in my entire life. I don't even like strawberry pancakes. And I especially didn't like that I copied Dave. *Way to establish yourself as your own man who is ready to start an adult life with this man's beloved daughter.*

But it couldn't get worse, right? I decided to get right to it. I'd ask Dave. He'd say yes. The pancakes would be celebratory.

Me: Dave, I'd like to marry your daughter and want your blessing.
Dave: Well, I think we should do the biblical thing.

(I grip my mug tighter)

HOW TO BE MARRIED (TO MELISSA)

Dave: I think you should work for me for seven years, and
then after that, you can marry one of her sisters.

You know that laugh you do when you're pretty sure someone is joking, but you're not 100 percent sure? The one where you're not even smiling and it's kinda a half-laugh noise on repeat? Like a laugh-stutter almost? I did that so loud that I sounded like I was what was crazy about Otto's.

As a comedian, I was conflicted. Jokes are great for breaking the tension, and this was a pretty good joke. For those who don't get it, in the Old Testament this guy named Jacob wanted to marry Rachel, so he asked her dad, Laban, for permission. But Laban said Jacob first had to work for him for seven years. Then, on their wedding day, Pops pulled the old switcheroo. The person hidden behind the veil was Rachel's sister, Leah. Because men could have more than one wife back then, Jacob had no choice but to work another seven years so he could marry Rachel too.

While it's not the most wholesome Sunday school story, there's a moral to it. What is it? Don't trust your in-laws. I mean, that might not be the actual lesson, but it's certainly my takeaway. As far as I'm concerned, it's in the Bible that God doesn't want us to trust our in-laws.

So Dave decides to (jokingly) offer me the same deal Jacob got. And while I adore Melissa's sisters, I wasn't thrilled with the offer. I politely declined. Eventually, Dave got to some of the standard questions I expected, and I pretended to have a plan for my life. Then he said yes in the same good-dad way he did in the church foyer years before: "I'll see if she's free."

Thankfully for me, she was. I mean, not literally. Melissa is actually very busy and doesn't allot downtime for herself and yells at me if I encourage her to take a break. But figuratively, she was available.

As Smooth As Cheap Whiskey

Of course, Melissa has done her fair share of cross-familial suffering too.

Believe it or not, I am not the only Nickerson to have seen Melissa naked. No, I share that distinct privilege with the matriarch of the Nickersons, my late Grandma Illa, the toughest woman I've ever known. No part of her wasn't rough around the edges. Her voice was raspy, her skin was icy, and she was mean. Grandma Illa rarely hugged you, and when she did, it didn't feel good at all.

Yet I knew she loved me. Despite every signal otherwise, I felt confident that this woman would do anything for me. She was a Great Depression kid whose life only got harder after World War II. She had five kids with a lumberjack who broke his back and then decided running underground gambling rooms was a suitable form of replacement income. Illa was cold but would do anything for her family, and her husband (the late Grandpa Jim) was the complete opposite: charming and cruel in equal measure. He'd butter you up and then beat you down. Illa endured through grit, self-sacrifice, and MacNaughton Canadian Whiskey. There's cheap whiskey, and then there's MacNaughton Canadian Whiskey. It wasn't bottom shelf. It was under the floorboards beneath the bottom shelf.

Illa was like many drunks and Nickersons (those words are synonyms) in that she started off as a happy drunk. She'd dance. She'd play Yahtzee. She'd reminisce about the good old days. But she would eventually hit a tipping point where everything became a lot less charming. For some people that's like three to four drinks in. But keep in mind, Nickersons don't have three to four drinks unless it's a short lunch break.

For Illa, the tipping point wasn't three to four drinks; it was more like 3:00 to 4:00 a.m. If she was still going at that hour, we knew she was going to be up for a few days. A bender, we affectionately called it.

Grandma Illa was present when Melissa made her inaugural trip to the Nickerson "lake house." I put that in quotes because I'm telling you right now, this lake house is not what you're picturing. This was not a million-dollar getaway cabin in New Hampshire filled with sweater-vests and mimosas. It was a simple house that my dad built on land my grandpa bought with the earnings from the aforementioned gambling ring. The house itself acted as the foundation of a seven-layer redneck dip that would be built around it. Trailers, horseshoes pits, a six-foot-tall garbage can exclusively for beer cans—you get it.

The days were spent fishing, swimming, playing in the field, and the kids desperately trying to find an adult not too hungover to take them tubing on the boat. The nights were full of fireworks, often literal, and sing-alongs, which around 1:00 a.m. transformed into what I call "fight-againsts," meaning instead of melodically singing with someone, folks were just yelling lyrics without a tune or harmony.

"The lake," as we called it, is special, and the first trip to Lakeside is a big deal—a rite of passage but fraught with danger. It's a lot like becoming a vampire: you have to be invited in, and most of the action happens at night. Melissa, adorable and naive, thought she would treat herself to a late-night shower at the lake house. She was due, after all. We had been swimming in the lake and broiling in the sun. She had a night sleeping on the ground in a tent ahead of her, so a simple pleasure was in order.

But showering is trickier than it sounds. On average, the Nickerson lake house would have thirty to forty people spread out between beds, cots, tents, and trailers—and just one bathroom. Plenty of places to lay your head, but only one place to shower in clean water, with soap if you were fancy.

The solitary bathroom had a lock, but it was considered a faux pas to use it. After all, someone (hopefully of your same gender) might need to enter and use the toilet while you were in the shower. (Of course, nobody would poop while you're in the shower. We were animals, sure. But, like, Disney animals. We have a sense of decency.)

There were unspoken rules for entering the bathroom when it was already occupied. Most important, you had to declare your intentions to the initial user. Usually there was a courtesy knock or an asking of permission or at least a loud clearing of the throat as a heads-up. But the rules did not apply to the Queen Bee. Illa would not knock or ask for permission. Such things were not required of her.

Melissa hopped in the shower at 11:00 p.m., seemingly a safe time for the uninitiated. But she forgot to factor in that we were on day three of an Illa bender (sounds like a type of lizard, doesn't it?). A rookie move if there ever was one. With no warning, Grandma Illa proceeded to barge in, leave the door open, pull down her polyester granny panties, and discard an unmentionable collection of noxious toxins into a toilet that she would not flush but rather leave for my adorable twenty-year-old Christian girlfriend. With Melissa petrified and trapped inside the shower, Grandma Illa sauntered out with a final word: "I don't even know who you are, so that's your problem."

Welcome to the family, Melissa.

Nevertheless, Grandma Illa did eventually forgive me for showering, and I learned to take military showers or just wear hats at the lake. She softened to me, and I'm sure the adorable great-grandchildren I later brought with me helped.

- - - - - - - -

Learning with the In-Laws

Even though I am still somewhat frustrated that I will never be the only Nickerson to see my wife naked, that's not the worst of the initiations. I wasn't the first Nickerson to kiss her. That's right. Uncle Butch holds that honor. The first time Melissa came over to my house, Butch planted a kiss on her before she could turn her head. Nonconsensual kissing is taboo these days, but back then it was how Uncle Butch kept the "fun" in "dysfunctional family."

If Illa and Butch weren't enough fun for Melissa, there's always fun to be had with my dad. For goodness' sake, we live with him now. Don is the sixth member of our household. My dad has lived with us for the better part of seven years now. He says he splits time between living with us and with my sister, Jessica, in Seattle. But being a Seattle native, I can tell you there are only three months you want to be there. Seattle is where parades literally get rained on. So it's not exactly an even split.

Jessica and I have always made jokes about which of us is Dad's favorite. But now that we are both adults, we know confidently: it's Melissa. Far and away, my wife is my dad's favorite child. And even though it hurts my feelings, I don't blame him.

I'd Like to Order a Happy Marriage. But Hold the In-Laws.

It's amazing how much you can tolerate family when you know they don't look down on you. That's where in-laws always break down. We have to be our own family, doing our things the way we want to. Grandpa Don meshes with our family because he brings what a healthy in-law relationship needs: no judgment and no agenda. The best in-laws just go with the flow of the family. They avoid being critical or intrusive. And they respect your boundaries . . . at least most of the time.

Being married to Melissa has taught me that every set of in-laws brings challenges. Your family may consider some things normal or even necessary that your spouse will consider maddening or even offensive. And when these tensions arise, you may feel ripped apart by loyalties. Both sides are your family, and both sides may feel betrayed if they think you've chosen the other.

The question is: Is your spouse worth it? Are they worth having to deal with the extra? Because you absolutely have to. There's no avoiding it. You can maybe do it less than others, but even when your in-laws aren't there, they're there. Holidays, vacations, Facebook fights, traumatic memories—they show up even when it's not an in-person sighting. Your family of origin shapes you in profound ways, and that doesn't vanish when you get married. It gets magnified.

For Melissa, I am worth it. For me, Melissa is worth it.

We've had spats and even fights over our in-laws. They've driven us to passive aggression or even aggressive aggression. We have had to draw uncomfortable boundaries with family members and even cut off family members multiple times until they started making better choices.

More than a decade ago, Melissa and I moved to San Diego (we "did it for the Lord," so we're essentially martyrs). Her family had already moved from Seattle, and now it was time to relocate away from my family. It wasn't that blatant of a decision, of course. We didn't decide we needed to be farther from them. But we sensed, even if it was subconscious or unspoken, that we needed distance to do our own thing well. If family was going to join us, it was going to be just that—*joining us*. Also, if you're not coming to visit us when we live in San Diego, do you even love us? It's friggin' San Diego! We've made this pretty easy for you.

Some marriages and families prioritize the extended family above all else. They spend their vacations with them; they live close to them; they build every aspect of their lives around them. God bless 'em, and no thanks. That ain't it for us. You can ride our bus, but we're driving, and you'd better not be too loud back there. Unless you're Grandma Illa, of course. She doesn't follow anyone's rules.

Chapter 4

Great Sexpectations

Before we kick this chapter off, I want to acknowledge that I know a lot of you skipped to this chapter to read it first. And not only do I not fault you for it, I applaud you. I'd be right there with you. It's an important and, frankly, a juicier topic. Personally, I would want to know an author's thoughts on this before anything else.

"So why not lead with it, Dustin? Why wait till chapter 4?"

Well, it's not like I've done studies about where to strategically place the most exciting chapters in a book so as to encourage people to read more of that book. It's not like I would intentionally withhold the sex chapter until chapter 4 so I could lure you in deeper and manipulate you to consume more of my content. Are you implying that? Because no, never. I would never do such a thing. Let's just say those other chapters were the warm-up act. Or perhaps I should say the foreplay . . .

And we're off.

Only You

Melissa and I have only ever had sex with each other. So I admit going into this, my advice is limited. Even telling people this often sounds shocking. Telling people you were virgins when you got married is like telling them you're from a different planet—but a way less cool one. But that's fine if you think less of us. If you didn't wait till marriage to have sex, that's totally fine with me too. No judgment here. To each their own. It's fine that you want to go to hell. Hope it was worth it. Two minutes for eternity. Good choice.

The fact that we had only been with each other caused the naivety that is the baseline of our story. A story that is about being young, dumb, and inexperienced. If there was a movie about those years of our sex life, it would a share a title with the hit '90s film *Clueless* (starring Alicia Silverstone and Paul Rudd, who somehow looks older in the movie than he does now).

(Scene cut to Melissa)

Melissa: *As if!*

When people find out you're marrying someone you've never had sex with, they get legitimately worried. They ask things like, "But what if you don't like it? What if you're not good together in bed?" Which, if you've had sex with multiple people, I totally get. That seems important. You'd want compatibility there.

One of my favorite comedians, Mike Birbiglia, has a joke about that where he said, "Sex is weird, you know? It's like tennis. You need to find someone of your own ability. Because if they're better than you, it's awkward. It's like their wailing the ball at you and you're like, 'I'm not getting anything over here! Do you like an underhand serve or a lob?'"[1]

Thankfully for me, Melissa was also bad at tennis. But good news? We could practice together. I cannot emphasize enough how dumb we were. You remember all those how-to books of the late '90s? *[Fill in the blank] for Dummies*, *The Complete Idiot's Guide to [whatever]*. Classic. Nothing inspires learning more than making someone feel stupid. Well, as a gag, someone got us *Sex for Dummies*, and you know what? It was *super* helpful. Because we were dummies. I was in college at the time and this was the only textbook I studied. Needless to say, there were a lot of "Ohhhh, that's what that does" moments those early years in our marriage.

Sex actually reminds me a lot of Legoland in San Diego. (I realize comparing sex to a children's amusement park is problematic. Stick with me.) When you walk into Legoland, you don't know what's there. They put you on a loop and everyone walks in the same direction. The first ride you go in is a dragon "roller coaster" that might be eight feet tall and go three miles per hour. I'm not even sure they need to strap you in. But you know what? It's the best ride in Legoland while you're on it. And you don't know any better till you get to the next one.

Melissa and I had no idea what we were doing, but we were having a good time. We were the two kids at the ice arena who didn't know how to skate but were having the time of our lives. Sure, our knees were scraped and Melissa sprained her wrist, but it's all smiles and we're getting hot chocolate afterward (because we weren't old enough to drink).

"Can You Relate?"

Sex is so personal that it can be hard to find people who relate to your own experiences. Even with married couples it's a challenge because (a) everyone's story is different and (b) the topic of how good (or bad) your sex life is doesn't just casually come up at the snack table during the PTA meeting. "Hey, let me cut you off there, Steve. I don't want to hear how things went with your wife in bed last night. She drives my kids to school every day."

The ones I can't relate to at all are my single guy friends, which as a comedian, I have a lot of. It's hard to communicate how different our lives are, especially on this topic. The point being, it's hard to understand and feel connected to others' sexual experiences. But hey, this book's whole premise involves not being relatable. So I'm off the hook.

But I do try to relate. When friends tell me stories of people they've been with in the past and how hard that can be, I try putting myself in their shoes. Comparisons, insecurities, the fear of what they aren't telling you . . . it's immensely challenging.

This was a gigantic part of the appeal of being with only one person. I'm so insecure I can't stand the thought of someone comparing me to someone else in bed. Because if you've never had sex, and if the person you're having sex with has never had sex, it will be the best sex you've ever had. From the start we were having a great time. We had no other experiences to compare it to.

Sex is the most intimate act in the world. It's vulnerable. It's passionate. It can be challenging and nerve-racking. But it's important. A 2015 study, based on data collected from thirty thousand Americans over forty years, showed that married couples who had sex at least once every week enjoyed "greater happiness" in their relationship than those who did not.[2]

Authors and gurus and horny couples with something to prove throw around numbers of how often you should be having sex. Of course, there's no number that makes universal sense for every couple. But once a week being a clear indicator of a happier marriage? Well, that proves that prioritizing it is crucial.

But we didn't know that. Again, we barely knew anything. And what I did know was wrong. Had I gone into our marriage with the same pure ignorance as Melissa, things would have been smoother. Like many married couples, we found sex to be fun and exciting at first, but then some of my past became my present.

A Pic in a Box

When I was ten years old, I found a *Playboy* magazine in our basement. Honestly, it was hardly even hiding—it was lying in an open box. I'm not sure that it wasn't left out on purpose. You know when you eat a bowl of cereal and don't clean the bowl because you know you're gonna use it again real soon? I think that was the idea my dad or uncle had when he didn't put it away. Regardless, this was a huge find for me. Pre-internet, porn was a real challenge to attain. It was easier to find a dead body than a naked one in the early '90s.

The first time I found the *Playboy*, I thumbed through it thinking, *Oh well, this isn't what I expected to find down here, but I'll respect it enough to, ahem, "read the articles."* But I was so mesmerized, probably by the searing cultural commentary and deft prose, that I left it on the counter. Yep, I discovered a stash of porn and then left it out in the open afterward.

HOW TO BE MARRIED (TO MELISSA)

We went camping that weekend and Uncle Butch asked, "Dusty, what do you prefer? Blondes or brunettes?"

Totally taken aback that Butch had shown any interest in my interests about anything, I responded, "Blondes."

"Then why were you looking at the brunette downstairs?" he asked.

For many families, Nickersons included, this was to be expected. Kids are naturally curious about naked bodies. That curiosity grows and is accelerated by exposure to pornography early in life. But what seems harmless at the time can often snowball and have negative ripple effects over time.

One run-in with a *Playboy* brunette at ten years old may not shock you. But that was just the introduction to the story. Soon after, I found a much more extensive collection of magazines at a different house. Then a few years after that, my dad bought a computer for our house. I was suddenly a highly pubescent boy with limitless access to every type of pornography you could imagine, and, as I've mentioned, almost no adult supervision. I was a kid in a candy store, only instead of sweets it was photos of naked women named Candy.

Listen, this is a comedy book so I don't want to dive too deep. But as I got older, things didn't get better. Porn was more than physical; it provided an escape. It's fantasy. You don't watch Harry Potter to learn how to become a wizard. You watch it to escape. With porn, you can create almost any scenario, no matter how unrealistic or unattainable. You can create scenarios that make you feel how you've always wished you felt about yourself: wanted, desired, valued. I'm not here to shame or put any type of moral judgment on anyone who looks at porn. I'm just here to talk about its effect on me and my marriage.

After I married Melissa, I realized that sometimes porn has the exact opposite effect on the nonusing partner. My porn habit made me feel more desirable, but it made Melissa feel less wanted. Suddenly, she was managing a psychological stress that she had never planned on. Melissa has always had a healthy self-worth, but this porn issue was stripping her of that. Recognizing this devastated me. It was not the type of stripping either of us had in mind early in our marriage.

Couple's Question!

What aspect of marriage were you most *wrong* about? What did you expect that didn't happen, or vice versa? For example, did you think there would be more sex and less fighting about whose turn it was to make the kids' lunches? Did you idolize marriage and feel surprised when you weren't happy all the time? Or maybe it was something less significant, like you just thought your spouse would want to play video games more often.

I needed help, but the help I had around me wasn't that helpful. We were actively involved in church circles, but if there's one thing that church culture is infamously useless with, it's helping people deal with pornography. I'm not blaming the church for my issues. Porn was my problem and my responsibility. But the church claimed to be a problem-solving resource—yet it only added more problems to the big one that I needed to solve. The purity culture I encountered recoiled from my porn habit and added guilt and shame more gross than anything I'd seen on an adult website.

HOW TO BE MARRIED (TO MELISSA)

Let me back up. I became a Christian when I was fifteen, about five years after I found that first porn magazine. I didn't know about the "no porn for Christians" rule until *after* I'd already been inducted (baptized). At the time, the rules for Christian teenagers were simple:

> Guys: Don't look *at* porn.
> Girls: Don't look *like* porn.
> Guys and girls: Don't *do* porn.

The emphasis on being "pure" and keeping yourself from any type of sexual sin was so prevalent in Christian youth culture that I started to think sex was all God cared about. It was at least in God's top three. So many youth pastors I knew built their entire ministry around it. Their check-ins would sound something like this:

Youth Leader Dude: Did you do it this week?
Youth Group Dude: What's *it*?
Youth Leader Dude: You know what *it* is.
Youth Group Dude: Oh. No.
Youth Leader Dude: Good job.
Youth Group Dude: Okay, but I lied to my parents, cheated on a test, and bullied a first grader.
Youth Leader Dude: That's fine. Jesus can overlook that. As long as you kept your pants on.

Then there were well-meaning pastors and leaders who quoted verses and told us to pray and read the Bible more. As a fifteen-to-nineteen-year-old male, the Bible wasn't always the most exciting pick for my evening literature.

Comedy Is Its Own Pleasure

Maybe God put me in comedy to help fill my need for validation. Turns out that having a group of strangers all sit down and listen to me—with the one rule being I'm the only one who gets to talk—helped with some control and self-worth issues that I'd struggled with when I was watching porn.

Performing at every different type of venue and show on earth, I interact with a lot of performers, including a couple of shows I've done with burlesque dancers. You know what's funny? They are there for the same reason I am: we're entertainers putting on a great show. The only difference is that no one in the crowd is hoping I'll take off my shirt.

Stand-up comedy is like personality porn. I'm showing you only the parts I want to reveal, and it's usually a distorted version of reality. You think I'm one thing, but I'm different in real life. It's part of my show. It's not that different from people's social media accounts, though—most people are posting updates only about certain parts of their lives.

Meek in the Sheets

Church aside, I knew I had to confront the porn thing if I wanted to be married to Melissa. It was crucial to realize that what happened with Melissa and I between the sheets was different from what I had seen. Our sex was different. It was real, it was intimate, and it was personal. It was two people in the real world doing real things. It was sometimes silly, often emotional, and always imperfect. Weird smells, uncomfortable questions, and stretch marks (which were all mine since Melissa hadn't birthed any kids yet).

This coincidentally helped me with a breakthrough that put porn in its proper place.

What I had experienced in church made me think porn was the biggest deal in the world. An unforgivable mistake, a sin I was enslaved to. It was neither. It was a thing I looked at every once in a while. It was something I took in during a vulnerable age of my life. It wasn't a non-thing, but it wasn't the biggest thing. Ironically, that's what helped me kick it—thinking of it as less of a big deal. But more important, it wasn't who I am. It wasn't my identity.

Another helpful reminder was that porn wasn't real life; those people were actors. The sex wasn't real intimacy between two people. It was scenes, a crew, call times, lighting, and a script. Those people on a set had errands to run later. I guarantee some of them are fantasizing midscene about getting Jack in the Box on the way home. Just humans.

We also had a hugely significant conversation with our friends Micah and Lindsey. They are a couple we love and respect, and we thought they could maybe help. It wasn't easy, but as we were all hanging out one night, I brought up pornography. Micah and Lindsey met us in that moment with such love, graciousness, and lack of judgment that it remolded our ideas of just how meaningful friendships can be.

MELISSA'S POV

Shout-out to Micah and Lindsey for being the friends we felt comfortable opening up to about this struggle. They didn't judge us, and once pornography was no longer our shameful secret, we found power over it.

— — — — — — —

As with all things, Melissa and I learned to communicate about our struggles but also about the things we liked. And yes, sometimes this included Jack in the Box. It wasn't always easy; openness takes effort. Rejection hurts. Sexual rejection is devastating. Not getting a Sourdough Jack when you want one may hurt most of all.

With sex, though, it feels like a rejection of both you and your body. Conversely, you can't expect all your needs to be met in the bedroom (or at the kitchen table, in the shower, on the kids' beds while they are at school, whatever). It's a delicate balance of being willing to ask but also being in a posture of giving. (And yes, posture of giving sounds 100 percent like a sexual position. I agree.)

You need to be willing to ask, willing to give, and also willing to be told no. There can be no demands. No expectations. Just an openness and understanding of what the other person is feeling.

Sex Hurdles

The longer you are married, the more obstacles to sex you face. And by obstacles, yes, I mean children. Oh, the irony that the product of having sex is the exact thing that prevents it.

There's no doubt that sex becomes more challenging for us as parents. Your wife is physically unavailable to have sex for whole seasons. The things that used to meet your sexual needs are now the source of your baby's food. It's a raw deal—almost as raw as the nipples the baby is chewing on.

Sex is made more difficult by a lack of sleep when the kids are young and then just a lack of opportunity as they get older. Kids stay up later and are more aware of all the happenings in the house. Sometimes I'm tempted to look at my son in high school and say, "Listen, you *could* stay up, but if you want to hold on to whatever remaining part of your childhood you have left, I recommend you retreat to your quarters."

Melissa and I both know that we have to put in the effort to prioritize sex in our marriage. This means setting aside nights to stay up later and know we're going to get less sleep. It means taking getaways without the kids, even if it's just an overnighter. It means taking lunch breaks and sending the kids to sleep over at their friends' houses. And it means never ever taking your kids to a wedding because (a) nobody wants your kids there and (b) we know we're going to go pretty hard at the hotel afterward.

MELISSA'S POV

When Dustin is in town, we make sex a priority. But when he is traveling, we are staying connected through texting, emailing, FaceTiming, and DMing constantly. Not just because we run a business together, but because we are lovers, partners, and best friends. He's my best friend who loses his belt, wallet, keys, computer, and phone chargers every two to three months.

— — — — — — — —

Overnighters are an important rhythm for us that an older couple modeled earlier in our marriage. They told us that once a month they get away for at least a night, and once a quarter they schedule a weekend away. That's not practical for everyone, but the principle certainly applies.

And in my experience, man, nobody goes harder in hotels than parents away from their kids. It's wild. That's why they are so important. You get to the room, you immediately shut those curtains, turn the lights off, get in that bed . . .

. . . and you sleep so hard.

I mean, it's wild. So many different positions. All night long. Sometimes you sleep, wake up, and sleep *again*. Sleep twice in one night? I mean, that reminds me of being a young man. Oh yeah, the sex is fine too. But the sleep is so good you're sore in the morning.

***

The bottom line is this: a healthy, safe, and passionate sex life is crucial to a marriage. But it doesn't just happen. It's the product of putting in hard work to understand yourself and your partner. Each of your desires, needs, and motivations have to be understood, and from that can flow the fun stuff.

And with that said, farewell to those of you who are only going to read this chapter. Again, I totally get it. Hope you enjoyed it, and sorry there weren't any illustrations.

Chapter 5

The World's Shortest
Advice on Cheating

We promised this book would not be generic advice and would draw only from personal experiences. I have never cheated, nor have I been cheated on. So in that spirit I can't speak much on this topic.

However, I know that cheating has incredibly painful ramifications. So if you're considering doing it, maybe don't? I mean, I certainly wouldn't recommend it. (How I really feel: quit being so selfish.)

And if you've been cheated on, I am very sorry and I cannot emphasize enough how important it is to seek help beyond this comedy book that was bought at the airport. Look at my ridiculous face on the cover of this book. Clearly, I'm not the guy to help. But Venmo request me, and I'll cover your first therapy session.

Chapter 6

Marriage Is About Balance, but Sometimes It Gives You Vertigo

Many popular things from my childhood have vanished over time. Rotary phones, Blockbuster Video, corporal punishment as the only acceptable approach to parenting—ah, is that a painful memory in the air, or just nostalgia? Hard to tell them apart sometimes.

But of all the things, ice cream trucks have managed to stick around. Yes, these child-abduction centers on wheels have stood the test of time. (And here I thought it would have been Pogs. You know, those small cardboard discs with cool designs that you could win your friend's entire collection of? Still surprised they didn't make it.)

Once upon a time, the whole concept of an ice cream truck seemed innocent enough. A nice man repurposes a vehicle, adds a cooler and fills it with sweet treats, and then cruises around neighborhoods to give the children the joy of buying a Choco

HOW TO BE MARRIED (TO MELISSA)

Taco—or the immense anguish of not being able to retrieve a dollar before the truck drove off, its blaring music slowly fading in the distance, teaching children the valuable lesson of always having cash on hand.

The modern ice cream truck is far inferior to the one I knew as a child—the prices are higher, the music is creepier, and the truck is only a day away from being featured in a true-crime podcast.

Growing up, nobody in my neighborhood had a lot of money, which is why the ice cream man didn't visit very often. Once, one of the neighbor kids asked him if he accepted food stamps, and we didn't see him again for six months.

When he did come, my sister and I often had to split something. Which is not easy. Ice cream and Popsicles are consumed by licking, and they can't be neatly chopped in half. This creates a scenario combining siblings' two worst nightmares: their mouths being close together and sharing.

(Music gently fades in) *"And then a hero comes along . . ."*

That is, except for one particular Popsicle with an added feature that allows it to be easily separated into two separate Popsicles when needed. Yes, the legendary two-stick Popsicles saved Jessica and me from many arguments and shared colds. I imagine that decades ago, a dad in some factory somewhere got tired of hearing his kids fight over Popsicles and decided to invent one that could be broken down the middle. Then, after that breakthrough, he spent the rest of his life trying to figure out how to split the rest of their things down the middle too. But alas, Cabbage Patch dolls and iPads don't cut as cleanly.

This splitable Popsicle is the single best metaphor I can think of to describe the need for balance in marriage. Melissa and I have learned that to stay married, we need balance. Specifically, equity, compromise, and a give-and-take approach to negotiating differences. And of course, sweet, sugary, frozen goodness.

Melissa and I joined together to become one married unit, one functioning organization, and even one bank account. A bank account that, at the time, looked like a rhinoceros foot (it had three digits). We know there's an important reason God put that whole "two become one" language in the Bible. But I am here to one-up the Lord with this killer Popsicle metaphor. You see, even though a couple becomes one, each person also has to retain a distinct identity with individual goals and purposes. It's a delicate balance. Otherwise, the couple becomes one of those boring Popsicles with just a single measly stick that sparks a lot of disagreement. (Take that, God—my analogy is way better.)

Maintaining that balance depends on strong communication. And communication requires two individuals equally committed to speaking and listening so each partner's needs are considered important.[1] Research shows couples who don't have balance are more likely to form resentment and tensions.[2] Being that I work from a baseline of resentment and tension toward all people, it goes without saying this is something that Melissa and I have had to work hard to establish.

Sticky Fingers

In our marriage, sometimes I end up with a little more Popsicle on my stick than Melissa does—both because I have the more forward-facing career and because I'm fifty pounds heavier and can handle the additional calories. Other times, Melissa gets the lion's share of the Popsicle, and I'm left holding the smaller side. And sometimes, it's hard to tell who is winning the Popsicle tug-of-war—all we know is both of us have sticky hands.

Activity Time!

How Do You Know If Your Marriage Is Out of Balance?

1. Do you like sharing things with your spouse? If not, what specific things do you prefer to keep to yourself? And we're not talking about food—nobody wants to share that. Is it experiences, emotions, money, or other, more serious items? These are important to unpack, to understand the *why* behind them. And then to talk to your spouse about— when the time is right. (But do so with the promise of shared *Schitt's Creek* and Ben & Jerry's afterward.)

2. Are you envious of your spouse's life? And by "life," I mean the day-to-day tasks on which they spend their hours. Do you wish you could swap places? This is a serious question in a comedy book, so if the answer is yes, look at the person, tell them you love them, and also tell them that they are the designated driver for the next month.

3. Do you fantasize about being alone? If yes, what level of alone? Are you envisioning an afternoon, a week, or the rest of your life? If it's not for the rest of your life and you're feeling a strong need for some alone time, then look at your spouse, say "I love you," and then go binge a half season of *Schitt's Creek* and a half-pint of Ben & Jerry's.

You might think that traveling for a living while my wife stays home with the kids is a sweet deal. But it's not all champagne bottles and turndown service (it's literally never that). It's actually airports, hotels, Lyfts, and—when I'm lucky—a greenroom with a space heater. This is the road life I've chosen, so I won't complain about it. But the having to deal with strangers part? That I will absolutely complain about. And it's not just strangers. It's strangers constantly asking the same predictable, boring questions:

- "You're a comedian. How'd you get into that?"
- "Who are your favorite comedians?"
- "How do you come up with your material?"

Or sometimes, they just say, "Oh, that's surprising. I wouldn't have ever guessed that from you." Which is less of a statement and more of an insult. Regardless, the questions strangers ask me are about as fun to answer as a census questionnaire. That's why if I don't have to tell someone that I'm a stand-up comedian, I don't. There are approximately five hundred Uber drivers across America who think I'm an event planner, which is at least 10 percent true.

Once they find out I'm a stand-up, they usually ask the same stuff. Every so often, though, the questions can lead to heavy conversations. They start asking the harder, knife-to-the-heart questions about my marriage and family:

- "Does your wife support your decision to do stand-up comedy?"
- "How are you able to pay your bills?"
- "How much therapy do you think your children will need as a result of your career choice?"

And the most common family question: "Is it hard on your wife and kids that you travel so much?" (One-star review, no tip.)

These questions feel like someone punched me in the gut and then stayed around long enough to ask if it hurt.

Yes, of course traveling is hard. As I'm writing, I've slept in six different beds the last eight nights. If it wasn't hard, it would indicate that Melissa and I have even deeper issues than we know about. If Melissa and the kids were thrilled every time I left, there would be no reason for me to come home.

Dustin Interrupts Himself

Travel is immensely challenging but in and of itself, it's not the problem. It just reveals the problem. It's like a leak in the roof. You don't know there's a hole in the roof until it starts to rain.

If you're struggling with feeling close to your partner, spending six nights a week fifteen hundred miles apart isn't gonna help. If having an active sex life is the issue, being apart won't make that any easier. And if one spouse thinks they are doing the bulk of the housework, well, leaving the home is probably the absolute worst thing to do.

For me, traveling exposes some straight-up, good old-fashioned sadness. I miss the kids, and they miss me. I deal with drunk hecklers and with idiots on airplanes, and I nearly have an existential crisis every time the hotel door closes behind me. You ever notice that half of Christmas songs are about musicians trying to get home for Christmas? When the other half are about the birth of Christ, that tells you it's pretty weighty out here.

And it's no picnic basket of happiness for Melissa either. She is often stranded at home by herself—well, my dad and the kids are there, too, but I think being by herself is easier than that. She has to sleep in our bed alone more nights than she'd like. She does most of the chores without my help, which means doing endless loads of laundry and nobody to share a glass of wine with. It's much harder for her, I think, which makes it even more emotionally taxing for me. I feel people's feelings. It's like telepathy except I don't get to be in the X-Men. When people are upset, I'm upset. And I often blame myself and feel guilt.

Bottom line: I'm not happy when people I love aren't happy, especially Melissa.

People also ask a lot, "Do you bring your family with you on the road?"

Oh, wouldn't that be nice. Of course, I am much happier on the road when Melissa is with me, but that's not always possible for us. But we have learned that bringing her when we can is important to our balancing act. It's always fun but requires sacrifice. It costs more to bring her, I tend to be (ahem) less focused on my job, and perhaps the biggest sacrifice of all is leaving the kids with their grandpa. I mean, who knows how much that actually costs us in future therapy sessions?

Country Mouse

It's always fun—and funny—when Melissa can travel with me. Because she has spent the majority of the last fourteen years immersed in the day-to-day lives of our kids, she sometimes forgets how to leave. Remember that old fable of the town mouse and the country mouse? It's the story where the simple country mouse comes and visits the cousin town mouse, who shows his country cousin around the city. Except the country mouse is Melissa—minus the cousin part. I'm not that kind of redneck.

The last time Melissa joined me on the road, we went to Nashville for our friends Aaron and Lucy's wedding, which I was officiating. (Remember, former pastor here.) And let me tell you, I *crushed* at that wedding. One of the best sets I've ever had. Aaron is a comic and Lucy manages a comedy club, so there was a ton of comedy types there and even they were laughing. I've still been meaning to apologize to Lucy for being the focus of all the talk at her wedding.

Melissa flew out on Southwest Airlines, so it started humbly, but on the way back we splurged (got a free upgrade) and flew in Delta One, the highest level of first class. Up there, you don't just get a seat. You get an apartment. Here's what you need to know about Delta One: You walk onto the plane and turn left. Nobody takes a left except the captain and 1 percenters. Our seats fully reclined so that we essentially could lie down, and we had our own at-home entertainment system. We were given free noise-canceling headphones and unlimited food and drinks.

It all goes to your head so fast you no longer even respect the captain. *Don't tell me what to do, buddy. You're just my sky Uber.* I expect a hot towel and a warm meal, STAT. And then once I finish that meal, I would like to be tucked in and sung a lullaby. Then as we start to land, a hot coffee (with Baileys, ideally), fresh-squeezed orange juice, and some verbal affirmations to start my day.

It made no difference that we couldn't actually afford to

purchase a ticket for the seats we sat in. Melissa and I live pretty modest lives, so experiences like this make us feel pretty important. And because I have no ability to remain humble in situations like this, I started referring to people riding in coach as the common folk. If the plane was going down, the back half of the plane would just break off and the first-class cabin would transform into a mini plane and land safely on a private runway near a five-star resort. We were needed as valuable contributors to society. Coach was just deadweight.

Every once in a while it's good for couples to feel better than other people. But Melissa and I try to keep our balance. When she travels with me, it's like she is getting a little more of the Popsicle on her side of the stick.

Cutting Yourself Off

Because of my career, that balance usually leans more in my direction, so we have to be intentional about empowering Melissa to follow her pursuits whenever I can take the support role. Last summer when she had an opportunity to teach an art class at a nearby, lower-income school, I stayed home to pinch-hit for Melissa.

Now, there's usually a reason that someone is a pinch hitter and not in the starting lineup. Namely, they aren't as good as the starter. Dad duty includes all the same tasks as Melissa would do, just slightly altered.

- Cooking meals = ramen and Honey Bunches of Oats (a better pairing than you'd think)

- Getting the kids to their activities = dropping them off ten to fifteen minutes late without a coat or both shoes
- Doing the household chores = frantically tidying up when Melissa tells me she's on her way home so she doesn't walk into a house that looks like it got hit by a cyclone

MELISSA'S POV

I love Dad duty even though Dustin writes jokes and makes TikToks instead of doing laundry. Everything doesn't get done the right way—*I mean, my way*—but that's okay. Dustin is also great at delegating as the kids get older, and though things are more prone to breaking, it's absolutely worth it. We only have so much time. Your teens and tweens can do the dishes!

- - - - - - - -

This experience taught me something: One parent having to deal with the majority of the household tasks is constant pressure. When I'm on the job, the work turns on and off. Life at home does not. There are always needs to be met and fires to extinguish. It can feel like you're a dry sponge that your roommates keep trying to wring out. And all the sponge wants to do is soak itself in wine.

It can also feel like parenting and household tasks are your entire identity. That's all you do, and therefore that's who you are.

I imagine Melissa saying, "Wait—didn't I go to school? I have skills, right? I didn't have a successful career to get good at making dentist appointments for everyone. And though I'm not sure if I would make more money than him, it's impossible for me to make less."

When Melissa was working, giving her talents to the world, we shifted the balance in her direction. What the act of her going back to work meant was just as important as the act itself.

In our marriage, balance can be as simple as one person gets to leave the house. One person gets to have a grown-up activity. One person gets to interact with other adults in a setting that doesn't involve Goldfish crackers. For many marriages like ours, one person ends up doing more at home than the other. But we realize Melissa cannot be in that role without time for herself. This is a disservice to her and to a world beyond our children that deserves her passion, gifts, and talents. But it's also a disservice to me because I like hanging out with my kids. Compared to my comedian friends, they're actually pretty mature.

An . . . Unusual Work Dynamic

Our marital balance includes creating wins that we share together. This became even more important after a fateful conversation I had with an older comedian.

Comedians talk a lot on the road. We're a tribe that understands one another. Most comedians talk about how, when we found comedy, we also found a community, a group of people who think and talk like us. We finally found other people willing to joke about literally anything at literally any time. We don't tend to fit in at most brunches and book clubs.

Because of that closeness there's a real vulnerability as well. We know we all have unique struggles, but they are shared. And I savor when I can find another married comedian who's trying to make his marriage work.

Once a comedian friend's marriage was near a breaking point. He had been on the road for decades, and even though his career had never been better, his marriage had never been worse. I listened to him and his wife fight over the phone once, and we processed it for hours afterward. I remember hearing her say something that I've always feared Melissa would say to me: "I do everything just to support you and your dream." This kind of statement is an indication that your Popsicle isn't splitting equitably, and something needs to change.

Selfishness doesn't usually show up with fanfare. It creeps in over time. I've worked hard at comedy, but I have to be ready to give it up if it's not sustainable for my family. Melissa and my kids can't suffer just because of my need to tell mediocre jokes at a divey comedy club in Wichita. (*That's not what's happening already, right?*)

This older comedian told me that even though he makes good money, and they live in a bigger house, and he's home more often than he's ever been, their relationship had been better in the earlier years because she had been more involved. Launching a comedy career is a group effort. As a new comedian, he needed help and his wife filled in. But as his career grew, he hired people to do what she used to do, which he thought would make her life easier. Instead, it kept them more separate and they didn't have balance. Eventually they made a change. They rearranged their marriage so that today, they are doing well. This course adjustment is what actual marriage looks like. In that moment, I learned so much about not just the struggle that marriages can have, but what it looks like to fix it.

Getting to watch and talk to this couple gave Melissa and me an important course correction, which was to involve Melissa as much as possible in my comedy career. Out and about I am a stand-up comedian, but at home Melissa and I run Dustin Nickerson Comedy. I'm the CEO; she's the CFO and the boss of the CEO.

Soon after COVID-19 hit, most live entertainment shows were canceled, including mine, so Melissa and I knew we had to figure out a plan. My plan was Melissa keeping us alive. Melissa's plan involved many things: saving money on insurance and applying for unemployment, grants, loans, and anything and everything she could. She got a lot more money out of the government than I did out of my dumb jokes that year.

Melissa's good at her job. She works tirelessly and is in charge of the money, branding, our Patreon (if you're reading this in 2091, Patreon is a members-only content platform), and merchandise. We do a weekly podcast together, and she handles our weekly email blast and my website. She offers tons of creative input and handles much of the decision-making. In some ways she runs the business, and I'm just the product we're selling. She is not the support beam of my dreams. She's my "damn CFO" (her words, not mine).

We both know that our marriage cannot be one-sided, with just Melissa supporting me and my endeavors, or vice versa. It has to be us as a team together, even when we aren't physically together. This is why when we are together at one of my shows, I make it a point to introduce her as my wife and CFO. Don't think for a second she's just some comedy wife. I'm not convinced this woman won't fire me if she has to.

Shared Wins

Melissa is great at her job but a tough coworker. She's mean, bossy, insulting, and demanding. We argue over decisions but also have the type of "meetings" that would be frowned upon in most work settings. It's an interesting dynamic. Neither of us have ever had more demanding jobs than the ones we have right now. The better a comedy career gets, the more pressure there is. The more eyes, the bigger the projects, the bigger the risks, the more things to balance.

MELISSA'S POV

Running a company with my spouse means not padding feedback as much as I probably should. Or at all. I'm trying to improve. I've told Dustin that I am really critical of myself, and my perfectionistic and unrealistic expectations can come out sideways on my loved ones. That doesn't make it okay, but maybe it helps if he knows where these mean words are coming from?

- - - - - - - -

Yet today our balance has never been better, and therefore, our marriage has never been better. We both have clear work and a purpose. We know that when the business wins, we win. When the kids win, we win. These are shared wins that have to be created.

This behind-the-scenes role fits Melissa. She doesn't need attention, but she needs to be involved. It doesn't have to be public, but it has to be present.

Melissa's not shy, by the way. If anything, she's an oversharer and tends to drop too much. This is the kind of interesting stuff that keeps me endlessly fascinated by her. She'll push to have her name and face on the cover of a book but doesn't want a public Instagram account. Why? Your guess is as good as mine.

MELISSA'S POV

I did *not* push Dustin to write a book about me or to put a picture of me on the cover. But I am flattered and it's a gift. This book has taken me way out of my comfort zone, in a good way. I absolutely could stay behind the scenes, but I think the world gets a more holistic view of Dustin when I'm in the mix too.

- - - - - - - -

Safe at Home

The flipside of the business is the house, and this is where I have to work to make sure I'm carrying some of the weight. We run the business together, but Melissa runs the home and sometimes I'm her hired help.

And I admit, I am not *good* at being hired help. If Melissa could leave a Yelp review on me as a household helper, it would have negative stars. Which is why when I'm "helping around the house" it tends to be kid focused and not task focused. Translation: "Dustin, entertain the kids so I can get some work done."

For the record, this is the 100 percent correct decision. If you've ever seen me try to fold a shirt, you'd want me as far away from the laundry as possible. Truly, a blind gorilla could fold at the seams better than I could.

Melissa actually has the house so much on lockdown it's hard to get anything done for her. Last year our youngest daughter, Claire, and I got Melissa some birthday gifts, but then we couldn't find the gift bags, wrapping paper, or even tape. Whoops.

She's also highly organized with the files, calendar, appointments, and dates. We've always joked that if we got a divorce, Melissa would have to serve me the papers, fill them out for me, and remind me of the court date. Honestly, she'd probably have to drive me, too, because she's better at directions.

This is where roles are very important. But not the roles that your parents had or the ones your church told you about—the roles that work for you and your marriage. Find the things you're each good at and then use them to serve the family together. Work from your strengths, desires, and gifts.

One house thing I'm great at? Planning the vacations. I travel for a living. I can crush that. Melissa hates research, but googling random things "to do" is an ADHD man's dream. Melissa planned the senior prom for her high school, and I planned her date with me. This perfectly encapsulates the two of us. Melissa can plan big things and execute something for a lot of people with a lot of details. Me? I can plan something great for the people I care about. Most prom nights include things like a fancy dinner, a carriage ride through the city, the dance itself, dessert, maybe a surprise private showing of a movie at a theater. Yeah, ours had all that. Not bad for a seventeen-year-old working with limited funds from my job at the movie theater.

But now that we're adults, our lives have changed, of course. For the better, but not because life in general is better. It's because we're better as people. We've matured, and we have perspective (and hopefully money). People often look down on young people. I do. But I know it's not because they're young. It's because we're jealous. We want our brains and bank accounts to be back in our twenty-three-year-old bodies. George Bernard Shaw reportedly said something to the effect of "Youth is wasted on the young."[3] I know that to be true because I was too stupid to not like George Bernard Shaw when I was young and forced to read him in school.

These days it is much more difficult to plan. I'm usually just trying to survive by playing it by ear. Three kids, a career, a marriage, aging parents: I've had to accept that I can't plan everything—or even a few things. I often don't know what's going to happen, and even more important, I can't plan how things are going to affect me.

For example, I might have a manuscript due in early June 2021. And I might be a procrastinator, hypothetically, but I know I'm a good one. I know I'll hit my deadline, I've never missed one, and besides, I put out my best work under the gun.

Then, in late May 2021, I got a concussion in a game of tag with my daughter because I am overly competitive. Yes, that's right. I hit my head too hard on the underbelly of a playground structure.

This led my daughter and me to return home and Melissa and me to discuss if I should go to the ER. We were chatting in our bedroom and I was eating a leftover salmon rice bowl from a big outing at Dave & Buster's the night before (sorry to flex like that). As I was trying to retell the story, I said the same sentence ten times in a row. My brain was on a loop. Melissa sensed my panic and we both agreed it was time to go to the ER.

Melissa's and my powers as a couple shine in the ER. She has all the cards and paperwork ready to go and understands where we need to be. I know how to emotionally work someone and just the right things to say to get us to the front of the line.

Thirty minutes later we're talking to the doctor. I told him the story of me saying the same sentence ten times in a row. Melissa chimes in, "Actually he didn't. He thinks he did, but he had actually just gone blank and stopped talking."

I had no idea my brain had created its own virtual reality and was projecting things that didn't happen. Two hours, three scans, and six staples later, we were out of there.

Post concussion proved to be a real challenge. Writing a book when your vision is blurred and your eyes hurt when you look at a computer is not ideal. I was in a delicate state for over a month. This was a real challenge because it's not like Melissa can step in and do my part of the job.

But she sensed the Popsicle was uneven and moved into high gear. When I was having panic attacks, she was there to talk me down. When I was stumbling over sentences, she knew not to point it out because that would upset me more. She knew the gigs I had to cancel and the ones I needed to keep. She stepped in to help in every way she could. She did some of the work, but she did something even bigger—she preserved the rest of us.

We made it through. My head wasn't permanently broken, and neither was our Popsicle.

Chapter 7

Our "Footprints in the Sand" Are on Different Beaches

F aith is important to both Melissa and me, and we knew early on that we wanted it to have a critical place in our marriage and future family. We value the virtues of justice, mercy, and humility, and we wanted our kids to have a reverence for the Lord and a love for other people.

And of course, who wants to sleep in on Sundays when you could get up even earlier than normal? Football, rest, food, and videos games for the kids? No way! Give me an eight-minute "modern" rendition of "How Great Thou Art." Kids love hymns!

For some, faith and religion aren't part of their marriage. But studies have shown that marriages with religious differences are "generally more unhappy, with lower rates of marital satisfaction" and also are "more unstable with particularly high divorce rates."[1] So for many, faith is not only an issue, it's *the* issue.

Though we were united religiously when we married, Melissa and I had very different routes to get to that point. As a family our faith practice has also gone in different directions. In fact, our journey together has been about as bumpy as the back of the church van where Melissa and I first met—on a youth group trip. Like Rihanna, we found love in a hopeless place.

A Pew Good Men

Melissa grew up in the church. And I don't mean a little churched. I mean Baptist Churched, which is way more intense. If Christianity is a light snack, Baptist Christianity is *Fear Factor*. She was in deep too. Her family is on an extra level of conservative, if you know what I mean.

Some of Melissa's family members are the level of conservative that if they were too much further to the right, they would get kicked off Facebook. For what it's worth, the exact same level of extra happens with liberals as well, but those people aren't going to get kicked off Facebook because they're too young to be on Facebook. And personally, if they're that kooky I wouldn't want them kicked off because my favorite form of entertainment is Facebook fights. It's what got me through the pandemic. Especially ones with family members. They're so rich because they aren't even about the issue. These people just don't like one another, and they both have so much personal dirt on the other person.

Once I was watching two cousins debate the vaccine, and it ended with one commenting, "You know what, I'm glad you didn't get custody of your kids." I sat back and enjoyed the show. (If this had been said between strangers, I would have been appalled. But since it was my family, it was easily the best movie I've seen in years.)

As a reminder, Melissa's conservative family was also an Air Force family, which means they bounced around the country and even did a three-year stint abroad in Japan. But no matter where they went, they always seemed to find a version of the same little Baptist community church. What were they looking for in a church? For a lot of folks, it's the preaching, maybe the music, maybe the doctrine. Melissa's family? Nope. None of that factored into their decision-making even a little bit. They were looking for one thing and one thing only: the strength of the AWANA program.

I realize that many people may not be familiar with AWANA, which is proof enough for me that God is real and merciful. If you're one of those blissfully unfamiliar readers, congratulations. That means you're the opposite of sheltered.

A quick overview: AWANA stands for Approved Workmen Are Not Ashamed, which is based on a verse in the Bible you're probably also unfamiliar with (2 Timothy 2:15, for those who are curious). The AWANA program was developed in the 1950s, so you know it's somehow less culturally relevant than the Spice Girls. AWANA is based mostly on rewards and merit badges for Bible memorization, which means it's also the program your kids will never beg to join. Instead of getting patches for knowing how to tie a nautical knot or carve an arrowhead, they offer rewards (aside from the ones stored in heaven) for reciting Bible verses.

In other words: Cub Scouts + Jesus = AWANA.

AWANA encapsulates a segment of the Christian faith that Melissa grew up in and that I later joined her in. The emphasis was on knowing the truth and being able to articulate it. This wasn't in opposition to feeling and living the truth, but the idea was that the actions and emotions would flow from knowledge. Knowing the faith was the most important part.

This works for a lot of people, and I won't knock it. But for young, little aspiring artists with rebellious spirits like Melissa and me, it could only take us so far. To her credit, Melissa finished the entire AWANA program. Most kids age out by junior high school (if not for embarrassment alone) when they are halfway through the Old Testament, but if there's one thing Melissa isn't, it's a quitter. On the other hand, I went to church one time as a kid and, coincidentally, it was for a single night of AWANA. I can't recall the circumstances that led me there. That's a big part of being raised by a single parent—you just kind of end up in a lot of places you're not familiar with, but you're there because your only parent is busy, and these places offered something loosely approaching "adult supervision."

I loved AWANA at the beginning. And by the beginning, I mean the first hour, when we just played games. I was seven. Group games were the pinnacle of my existence. Is this what it meant to be God's people? Giant games of Sardines? Then all God's people said "Amen"?

Unfortunately, then it was time to recite Bible verses, and the honeymoon was over. Reciting Bible verses from memory? I didn't even have a Bible in my house. I decided AWANA wasn't for me unless it was just going to be dodgeball followed by more dodgeball.

SK8 or Die

I wouldn't step foot into another church for almost ten years, but during that time, Melissa didn't miss a single gathering—Sunday morning, Sunday night, or Wednesday night. The day I finally returned to church, I didn't even technically make it into the building. I stopped in the parking lot because a traveling, Portland-based ministry called Skate Church (they dug deep on that name) was holding a skateboard demo / evangelical rally that day. Think Billy Graham meets the X Games. It was a skate-and-save spectacular.

Let me clarify, though, that when I say "skating," I don't mean skateboarding. Regrettably, I mean aggressive in-line skating. Yes, I Rollerbladed. Every day. For a long time. (And here you thought you couldn't respect me any less.) It was a trend that Christians couldn't resist because, for a brief moment in the last decade of the 1900s, aggressive in-lining was *somewhat* socially acceptable—or, dare I say, a little cool? My friends and I had fun years waxing curbs, repurposing handrails, and jumping over stairs. My knees, back, and wrists have paid the price for those years, but if there's one thing you can count on a teenage boy not having, it's perspective.

One note about Rollerblading: it's faster than walking, but not that much faster. Which means the options of where you can skate are limited. You end up visiting the same spots quite a bit, and if the janitors are there that day, suddenly you're down to even fewer spots.

Rollerblading was my life until the Disney Channel slammed that door shut in the most public fashion possible—with the release of the 1998 movie *Brink*. (Nothing says "the movement is over" quite like an after-school movie on the Disney Channel.) But before that movie, I met Micah. No, not the book of Micah. A slightly older boy named Micah who had a car and shared my love for being an eight-wheeler. And yes, the same Micah from Micah and Lindsey. And now you have Micah's origin story.

Micah was friends with my sister, and to this day he's genuinely the nicest person I've ever met. I've never had a friend that I make fun of more consistently, and yet he laughs harder every time I do. This is the ideal friendship for a future stand-up comedian. (And if Melissa didn't like when I teased her, our relationship would have lasted even shorter than Rollerblading being cool did.)

Micah and I skated a lot, and one day he worked up the courage to do the thing every good youth group kid is supposed to: invite me to church. Since it was for the aforementioned skate rally, I thought, *Sure. Why not? I like skating, I like Micah, and if this place will have more Micah and more skating, I'm in.*

So I joined Micah at church and two significant things happened. First, I became a Christian. Second, I badly failed a spinning 540 attempt on a half-pipe in front of a lot of people. Both ended up leaving permanent scars.

At the end of the skate church rally, a guy jumped through a ring of fire and gave some sloppy message on Jesus leading us through the fire. It was a little bit Jesus, a little bit Johnny Cash, and I decided to bite. This church had a great AWANA program, so—spoiler alert!—Melissa's family was there too.

After I got "saved," I joined the youth group and became the youth-group poster child. I was cool (by youth group standards at least), I played bass guitar in the worship band, and I had "a testimony," which back then was code for "didn't grow up with all this Christianity and smoked pot a couple times." Melissa was a fringe youth group kid. She was busy with school, sports, working—you know, stuff that isn't church on purpose. This was probably her least "Christian" phase of life.

A couple of years into loosely being around each other, Melissa and I ended up in the back of that church van on our way to a rural mission trip at a small town in Montana. Our youth group was responsible for doing yard work, buying groceries, some small community events, and chopping wood and delivering it to homes, which would provide heat for the winter.

On this trip I remember a couple of distinct moments that attracted me to Melissa and showcased some of the things I still love the most about her. In the field where we were chopping wood, the adults operated the chainsaws, the boys swung the axes, and the girls picked up the chopped wood and stacked it. We all had roles that worked to get the wood to people's homes in the most efficient manner possible. Over the course of that week, Melissa was the one girl who didn't demand to swing the ax. All the other girls did, and they weren't strong enough. They would miss the wood. They usually didn't even make a dent, and it would slow the work down. Melissa never asked to swing the ax and didn't seem to have any interest in doing so. True confidence is having nothing to prove.

One afternoon I specifically remember many of us were splitting wood and Melissa was working with the kids in the community at the church next door. I looked over at her and saw her dancing with the kids attending vacation Bible school. She was so silly and free and didn't care what other people thought. Melissa, in that moment, was what she always is: 100 percent herself and never pivoting according to what others want from her. I don't know of a single better attribute a person can have. We wouldn't get married for another three years, but I knew I'd found my wife that week.

Melissa is nothing if not genuine. It's what I have always loved most about her. I admire it and aspire to it. It's the driving force of why we both are apathetic to celebrities, politicians, and, ahem, "some Christians." If it's fake, we want no part of it.

After that trip Melissa and I officially started dating, and I'm not sure I ever felt cooler than when I showed up at her school as the new boyfriend. She was a year ahead of me in high school, even though she's only four months older. Dating an older, popular girl that's from a different school? Jesus loves me, this I know.

For a little while, Melissa and I stayed at the church where we met, even had our wedding there. We became members. We served. But there were things that just didn't click for us. The longer we were there, the more we sensed a disingenuousness and a lack of depth. Then we saw hypocrisy and terrible character failings from some of the church leaders, both staff and volunteers, until we began to think our church experience as now-married adults was beginning to unravel our faith. Our faith changed; it wasn't the tidy little package it once was. It looked less like something brand-new you'd buy in the store and more like an Amazon package that the driver was particularly angry at. But I think this is an important part of faith in marriages: looking not only at the *what* of your belief but also the *why*. Often the *why* tells a more important story that helps you understand each other on a much deeper level.

That wasn't our last challenging experience at a church. Melissa's conservative upbringing in the faith, my lack of upbringing in any faith, the dysfunctional church experiences we were a part of and contributed to—all of those affected our marriage. We've spent many years acknowledging and trying to understand that many of our religious experiences clashed and enhanced one another. In good ways, in bad ways, and in a lot of ugly ways.

Life on Mars

When we moved to Seattle proper, we found the opportunity to leave the church, but that led to one of our first married fights. Melissa wanted to switch to a closer church. I wanted to go, too, but people liked me at the church we had been going to, and I had (still have) a crippling need to be liked. But since the first church was far from where we'd moved, I caved pretty easily. Nothing like a commute to blame for leaving your church. "It's not you, Pastor; it's the traffic."

Religion has the potential to be the biggest point of tension in any marriage. This makes sense, right? Because even though money discussions can be tense, they pale in comparison to "I think your mom is going to spend an eternity in hell" discussions. Because of the nature of religion and faith, the weightiness of the questions they strive to answer, and their potential ramifications in daily behavior—I can think of no issue in marriage with greater ramifications. "Hey, what time do I pick up the kids, and do you think God is real?"

By no means does this imply you have to agree on everything. That's impossible and not even remotely healthy. But you do have to be open and you have to discuss it. You can't have an agenda to convince the other spouse to join your team, and you can't make isolated decisions on how to raise the kids.

Melissa and I have had more than our fair share of disagreements over religion, the Bible, prayer, and their impact and execution in our family. But I look back on that first little fight, and it might have been the last time we had a disagreement to do with our faith. Since then when we disagree, it's not a debate—it's a discussion. And I think that's the key. Because faith is so personal, it's easy to feel attacked and condemned when someone as close to you as a spouse has contempt toward you. Our faith is not something we do; it's who we are. People don't just practice Islam; they *are Muslim*. It's an identity, so in a marriage it has to be handled delicately with the utmost love and respect for the other person.

Our new church was called Mars Hill Church, which was then pastored by a guy named Mark Driscoll. If you've never heard of either, well, enjoy that Google search. Much has been said about Mark and Mars Hill, and even though this is a marriage book that is hardly even about marriage, it's also not the platform for a church scandal tell-all. But the circumstances that led us to Mars Hill and away from Mars Hill are pretty telling of our respective faith journeys.

Mars Hill represented a lot of things, but the main thing it offered us was that it was something different. It was cool, the music was loud, the preacher was funny, the walls were black, and it felt like Seattle. It felt like us.

When I say the pastor was funny, I have to be true to my job as a comedian and say he was funny only by pastor standards. Getting laughs as a pastor is the easiest thing in the world because it's not expected. Kinda like when a comedian makes a good point. When that happens, you should ask yourself, *Was it a good point or are my expectations for a comedian just low?*

We were young and Mars Hill was young. Going to church there felt like something we were doing together, which is an important ingredient in a budding marriage. Melissa and I are definitely not like-minded about everything, but we want to at least feel like we're going in the same direction.

Here's an anecdote that tells you all you need to know about why we made the change to Mars Hill. Our old church had spent the better part of ten years on a building campaign. Two weeks after it opened, they had a rule that you couldn't bring coffee into the sanctuary. It was blasphemous if you spilled on the new electric-blue carpet. A Sunday morning service in the Seattle area that doesn't allow coffee? I almost bought a robe just so I could tear it.

On our first Sunday at Mars Hill, not only were we allowed to bring coffee; the church provided it for free and it was *good* coffee. They didn't even care if you put a lid on it. That's the kind of reckless commitment to caffeine that'll make me take a membership class at a church.

At this time I was studying to be a sportswriter, but I was wavering. A professor told me, "One day you're going to wake up and decide you want to devote your life to something other than writing about sports." He was correct. I had grown up playing sports, knew I wasn't good enough to play them professionally, but decided maybe I could write about them. Seemed logical. But what the prof tapped into was the deeper issue: Was sports what I wanted my entire life to be about? The answer was no. Perhaps it was because I have a deep, philosophical soul and I wanted to put out work into the world that helped people. (Or perhaps it was just because I was in Seattle and spending a lifetime covering the Mariners felt like a prison sentence.)

Eventually this would lead me to comedy, where I could write and talk about anything I wanted. But I was young and Christian and in a cool, growing church, so I of course took it as a clear calling from the good Lord to become a minister. I switched my major to religious studies and became a ministry intern at Mars Hill. Then I became a youth minister and stayed for close to seven years. For the record, though, I was terrible at it. Why? Well, for starters, I don't like teenagers. And that's an important part of the job.

Don't get me wrong: I care about teenagers, but they're awkward. Especially middle schoolers. They don't really have a place in society. They aren't children, they aren't adults, and they aren't even really human. They're like tadpoles when they have the tail and the legs at the same time. In their perpetual discomfort, many of them are less than respectful to adults. Very few of them are cute; they aren't useful, they don't move right because they have no natural fluidity to them. I think the decision to make a middle school came from looking at the kids that age and saying, "Here, just go be weird together."

This irony is, this awkwardness is what makes a church youth group the perfect place for them. It was for sure invented by parents who looked at their middle school boy who smelled like the dumpster behind an Applebee's, and when they looked at their awkward baby with a mustache, they said, "This is God's problem" and outsourced him to the church. When I was in my tadpole years, it was a home away from home where people were kind, less judgmental, and seemingly interested in something other than themselves. That kind of comfort was hard to find back then, and almost impossible to find now as an adult.

But as a youth pastor, I basically fought the urge to say, "I love you; I would do anything for you; I would die for you. But I don't like the way I feel when you're near me." At that point in my life, I was doing most things for respect and validation. (And by "at that point," I mean every point of my life before and after that point, including the point in which I'm now writing this book.) And church offered another place for me to search for validation. Teachers and coaches may not like you, but I thought pastors had to. I'm older now, and my stance on teenagers has softened a little. But I wouldn't say it's changed. During the 2020 pandemic I had to do a gig for a youth camp two hours outside of Dallas, Texas. What a terrible energy for comedy—a bunch of sweaty virgins in the woods. I was there thinking that, best-case scenario, I was going to catch COVID-19.

Mixed Nuts

Back then Mars Hill had a culture of confident, macho, domineering-type men. I am not that, nor did I want to be that, but I did want them to like and respect me. I wanted to be affirmed by these older, "successful and mature" men who would say they were proud of me.

I was also attracted to being a pastor by the access to the pulpit, which is perhaps the single worst reason to get into ministry. I was drawn to the part of the job where I got to stand onstage and talk to people. But the challenges of ministry at Mars Hill were so great that I quit to give *stand-up comedy* a try. You know, the thing people are most scared of? The pressures around church circles makes everything so somber and serious and heavy and important—also known as everything I don't want my life to be about. I looked for redemption in making strangers take life a little less seriously.

I also got into ministry to help people, to feel like I was impacting lives and families and my community in a positive and lasting way. Did I do that? Yes, I'm confident of it. Did I do the exact opposite of it as well? Yes, I'm also confident of that. When you are young, inexperienced, insecure, and driven by a desire to be successful, you hurt people along the way. And by "you," I mean me, and after we left Mars Hill—and later, ministry altogether—I apologized and tried to reconcile some of those relationships.

Melissa and I were 100 percent sold out to being in church at Mars Hill for about two years. But around the two-year mark, seeds of disillusionment would be planted that informed our faith for the next decade. These were based on the pride and hypocrisy of leaders, people using the church for personal gain, highly questionable financial decisions, and what I would say now was just a general lack of interest in modeling a life that looked anything like Jesus. The coffee was good, but not *that* good.

MELISSA'S POV

I think one of Dustin's biggest strengths at Mars Hill was his ability to recruit and manage hundreds of volunteers. The church expected its members to serve like it was their part-time job. And these people were ridiculously kind, humble, and consistent. They showed up every Sunday morning to serve forty two-year-olds (all in one room, which is absolute chaos). We still keep in touch with a lot of these folks.

- - - - - - - -

This happens to a lot of couples. We've seen so many friends who never fully recover from these faith crises. It's hard to go through them alone, and it's hard to go through them together. For Melissa and me, we have spent the better part of a decade still discussing the ways the faith circles we were in during the early part of our marriage affected us. We've seen some who went through similar experiences, and they led to divorce. You can feel rejected, a failure, and isolated. The crisis can lead to arrogance and ego or shame and despair. The stakes are devastatingly high on faith and religion, and they need to be treated as such.

Wineskins? You Had Me at Wine

Melissa and I started a family while we were at Mars Hill. We'd bought our first home, the town house that lasted a little longer than one of Joel's longer naps. We'd planted roots, but Melissa and I also started having spiritual discussions that sounded a lot different from what was being preached. Because we're both action driven and had a heart for the needy and the least of these, we were feeling disconnected from the church's focus. Few churches, not just Mars Hill, do as much as they might want or say they do for less privileged people. When you look at their budgets, you see a different story. It's like looking at *my* family budget and saying we have a heart for eating healthy when, in reality, we have a heart for fish tacos and animal-style burgers from In-N-Out.

Then we moved to San Diego, which is where Melissa and I had a breakthrough. I was still working for a church (spoiler alert: there was good and bad from these years as well), but I got honest with her about something that would shape us forever: I told her I didn't want to be a pastor anymore.

I had been scared to tell her. I was scared of the judgment, and I felt ashamed and that I had failed. But I had grown weary of being a professional Christian. I hated having my faith tied to my job. I explained that I was tired of always having to *think* the right way. I was so much more interested in the *expression* of faith. Melissa responded with understanding and supported my making a change. Instead of my worst fears coming true, my openness led to a beautiful moment that opened the door for more conversations between us.

For Melissa, she started to talk about the language and packaging of the Christian faith. She disliked how people would just throw verses and catchphrases at us, expecting it to make things all better. I'd felt the same way but would have never known she was having similar feelings had she not told me. The old language is still a real challenge for us. Christianity does a good job of not even trying to repackage ideas and just throws the same terms around a lot. For creatives, this is less than ideal. Frankly, it can feel insulting.

Couple's Question!

What's one thing in your faith system that you've always felt uncomfortable about but have been afraid to tell your spouse? Think about it... then tell them!

One of my favorite sketch shows is *Portlandia*, which pokes fun at all the silly people who live in that ridiculous city. I know Portland well; it's like Seattle's younger brother who went goth for attention. It's as if a mason jar were an entire city. Truly, it's something special.

On the show there's a recurring sketch about two interior designers whose entire design scheme is about birds. They'd look at an item, especially if it was handmade, and say, "Put a bird on it," and—look!—it's better.

This is how Melissa and I started to feel about the church's use of Bible verses. Eating disorder? Put a verse on it. Depression? Put a verse on it. Addiction? Put a verse on it. Look—now it's better. It's patronizing anytime you feel like you're just a purse that someone is slapping a bird on.

The good news is when it comes to the Bible itself, it's a big book, so there's always something newish. Personally, I spend a lot more time in the emo Ecclesiastes stuff now because I relate to it a lot more. Don't tell me I'm being a downer because I think life is meaningless. It's in the Bible, in the Nihilism Testament.

Another thing that became an issue for us is that it seems a church's use of people is inverted. Melissa is a servant, but what the church offers her is a hospitality team and kids' ministry. That's what I did for years in my youth pastor roles, and we often needed someone to hold those babies and drive those youth vans. But Melissa, she serves widows and does their laundry and gives them rides to church. She brings meals to new moms. She teaches art to underprivileged kids in the community. The church doesn't have programs for that, so they don't have programs for us.

Because I don't really like small talk and chitchat, most church services are a straight-up nightmare for me. I like to spend my nights in comedy clubs with the funniest people on the planet, talking about life, comedy, faith, crowds, whatever. Melissa and I used to have a standing beer-and-quesadillas night after my weekly Tuesday show with my comedian friend Zoltan Kaszas. We called this Tuesdays with Zoltan (I told you we were creatives). Melissa often wouldn't say anything because she said it was so fun to just watch two comedians talk. It's like a heightened version of normal conversation. I do this a few nights a week, so yeah, a small group Bible study is a little slow for me.

For the record, I'm not against reading the Bible and Bible studies. Even though I feel like this is stating the obvious, according to my spectacular editor, Jenny, "For many folks, the obvious needs to be said." So here we are. Pro–Bible reading.

In our conversations, Melissa and I do wonder what others think of us. It's interesting to know that for some people, we are the most religious, conservative people they've ever met. We go to church; we take the label of Christian; we pray before meals. Full-on Jesus freaks.

And for others? We're prodigals who have abandoned the faith. You aren't members anywhere? You spend the majority of your time with non-Christians? I mean, when Jesus said he was the friend of sinners, surely he didn't mean that literally.

We're happy here. There was a time we pursued faith and

spirituality from the top down, from our brains out. Now it feels more like an inside out. We have become the opposite. We feel and live the truth more than we know it. The road is still bumpy, but at least we're the ones driving the van now.

What this led to is us being much more openhanded with our faith matters. We believe. We're on the team. But we treat church and Christianity much differently now. I often think about how in the early church, some people felt it was important to write down all the rules and beliefs. This group was all about knowledge, doctrine, and the creeds. At the same time, there was a group painting on the walls of the catacombs. That's what an expression of faith looked like for them.

Melissa and I are the tomb painters now. Our faith comes out through art, relationships, service, and our agenda. We'll attend a church and not sign off on their doctrine. We'll do things that some people in the church wouldn't even approve of. But that's okay. It's all one. We're all one. Is this a U2 song? It's starting to feel like it.

MELISSA'S POV

We're still working out our salvation with fear and trembling (Philippians 2:12). Ah, AWANA is still in my blood!

- - - - - - - -

Now, by "we" I mean mostly Melissa and the kids because let's be honest: I'm gone a lot on Sundays. If I'm home on the weekend, it's a welcomed break. If I'm home too many weekends, uh-oh, Dad isn't working.

Taking the kids to church solo is exceedingly challenging for Melissa. Our kids sit in the service and get bored. I can relate. Kids bored in church are like crying babies on planes. I feel the same way, but I'm not allowed to show it because unfortunately it's frowned upon to play *Angry Birds* during the sermon.

Melissa and I also both cringe at the parade of taking your family to church every Sunday. It's a good activity, sure. But often it starts to feel like the Westminster Kennel Club Dog Show, but for families. "Okay, my kids are well groomed, walk in a straight line, have clean teeth, and only talk when they're supposed to. Where's my blue ribbon?"

MELISSA'S POV

Taking Dustin to church involves stuffing my purse with a variety of mints, gum, fidget toys, notepads, and pens. And a couple of packs of surprise fruit-snack gummies I whip out toward the end of the sermon. He's allowed two bathroom breaks. It's best to confiscate his phone except when he's been gone too long on a break and I need to send a "get back in here" text. These tips help the kids as well.

Another wife/mom trick: if we leave for church early enough, we can get donuts or hot chocolate on the way.

— — — — — — —

Sometimes when we're around those old religious settings, it feels like what Jesus talks about in putting new wine in old wineskins. It doesn't sit right. It doesn't feel right. I don't want to say we've evolved, because that makes it seem like we think we're supe-rior. Though I would say we have changed for the better, it's *our* better. It feels right and we don't miss the past. As much fun as it is to log on to Facebook and see our old pastors rant about how it's fine that Trump said he could grab a girl by the [word this stand-up comedian isn't even comfortable saying] because at least he's pro-life, we're pretty happy here in this new wineskin.

When it comes to faith matters, Melissa and I learned we need to be brutally honest with what we're going through. If we've changed, we need to share that. And we need to be ready to hear that from the other person. People change, beliefs change, and the environments around us change. We've found we're often going through similar changes, which is great. (I've always loved when Melissa changes in front of me.)

Chapter 8

We're Both Fat, but Only One of Us Is Pregnant

Of course it's true. Everybody knows it's true. It must be true. Individual health is connected to the overall health of a marriage. Because of course it is. The better you feel about yourself, the healthier your relationships. It's just one less thing to be unhappy about and put on another person. Studies have proven that "healthier people may have a better chance of getting married and staying married."[1]

I've always known this in my heart but wouldn't admit it. Add it to the list of healthy things I refuse to digest. I think it's because I'm so turned off by healthy eaters. I like a lot of their food choices. I don't even hate their approach, usually. It's them personally I don't like. Because like a lot of people who get into a niche and drop into a rabbit hole and then oversell the weird thing they're into, they start pushing it on a level that sounds like Kool-Aid is on the menu. It's never, "Hey, I'm doing this new thing. It's worked for me. Maybe it'll work for you." Diet, exercise, astrology—they're all the same. It's too good to be true. They're the Star Wars prequels—even if it's good, it could never live up to the hype.

That being said, some fads are worse than others. In my professional opinion (I have a master's degree in not liking people), there are three primary culprits who are exceptionally worse than all the others. I am, of course, referring to CrossFit, keto, and essential oils—the unholy trinity of annoying things middle-aged, middle-class adults get into.

CrossFit might be the easiest for me to say no to because I straight up don't like the way they work out. Seems dangerous and hardly even like actual exercise. CrossFit was probably invented by a guy who grew up and really missed recess. "Okay everyone, today we're doing rings, hopscotch, freeze tag, and tires. But first, everybody line up for kettlebell dodgeball!" And the workouts feel like borderline chores. "Today's WOD (workout of the day): chin-ups, clean-and-press, and then everyone's gonna chip in and help me move my fridge."

Not interested.

Then there's keto, which I admit is a cool name. The word *keto* sounds like a *Pokémon* or *Mortal Kombat* character, both things I have interest in. And yet somehow, I still have zero interest in keto.

Crazy thing? I don't even know what it is. I think as soon as I hear the word, my brain just turns off and all I hear is Charlie Brown's teacher's voice. So I hate it, despite not knowing a single thing about keto and even though I've heard about it more than I've heard stories about my grandpa.

I bet I've heard two thousand pitches from the keet-heads. It's all they do. Keto is like the Jehovah's Witnesses of diets. And do they oversell it like those J-Dubs (yes, I gave Jehovah's Witnesses a nickname) handing out tracts in the '90s! "Can I tell you about my savior, Keto? He's helped me with everything. I'm losing weight, sleeping better, my kids are getting better grades, and he saved my marriage. Keto guides me beside distilled waters . . ."

But the granddaddy of them all is essential oils. Nobody on the planet is more annoying than the oilers. Listening to the multilevel marketing pitch of an oiler is a torture tactic that even Guantánamo Bay would consider excessive. Please just let me off the hook and waterboard me instead.

If you are an oiler, I know you're twitching for your vial as you read this. Thinking about how you'll baptize me in peppermint if you ever see me. Honestly there's a strong chance you're diffusing as you read this. And I don't judge you because, listen, I get it. Believing in magic is fun. I just need you to admit oils can't do *everything*.

If you're not familiar with essential oils, I'll fill you in: it's this small cult that thinks whatever your life problem is can be fixed by their magic oil. Their pitch goes something like this:

Oiler: Okay, just take this, rub it on your neck, and that'll be good for your skin and your dog's anxiety.
Normal Human: Really? Tell me more!
Oiler: Well, it's not supported in the medical community, because what do those nerds know? And it's a pyramid scheme! Keeps getting better!

I know a lot of people lost friends from online fighting over politicians and social issues, but I had already burned all my sage and bridges over essential oils. I went through a phase where whatever I posted, oils was the solution.

Me: I've got an upset stomach.
Oiler: Well, have you tried essential oils?

Me: I'm nervous about the current political state.

Oiler: Well, have you tried essential oils?

Me: I'm grieving the loss of a close loved one.

Oiler: Well, have you tried essential oils? We have a resurrection blend! We'll diffuse the funeral and see what happens. Worked for Jesus—Happy Easter, by the way!

Meat Me in the Middle

One of the things Melissa and I most have in common is our equal displeasure for extremes. We are truly moderates in almost everything. I can't think of a single viewpoint we have that is extreme.

Melissa has been able to maintain that moderation in her health. Good diet, steady exercise, some chocolate at night, go hard every so often, rinse and repeat. She has the steadiness of the pace car in NASCAR races. She's not gonna win, but she's not gonna crash either.

Me? Absolute madness. No self-control. I am all-or-nothing. Go big or go home. Or more accurately, stay home and eat big.

There was a baseball player in the early 2000s named Adam Dunn who was good at two things: hitting home runs and striking out. He hit over forty home runs in a season six times in his career. Very few players have done this. He also led the entire league in strikeouts four times. Even fewer players have done that.

This is me with eating. If I'm gonna get in the batter's box, I'm gonna take a big swing. Like a lot of people, food and my body and image are all tied into larger things in my life. My family is incredibly judgmental about weight. Both sides. Though my mom's side has kind of earned it. They tend to be leaner, good-looking, athletic types who won't outright tell you that you look fat, but they'll be quick to tell you if you look skinny. Especially too skinny.

They say things like, "Melissa looks skinny. Is she eating enough?"

Ah, there it is. The compliment-insult combo. Because we inflict trauma if we just let someone feel good about themselves, right? Isn't family the best?

My dad's side is where my genes come from. And these are the genes that have a hard time fitting into jeans. But not for one second does this stop them from being as judgmental as the jocks on the other side of the family. I remember one time, after not seeing me for a few years, I saw Uncle Butch at the lake house. Butch decided he wanted to let me know that he knew I had gained weight. His choice of greetings? "Oh, Dusty! You look . . . healthy."

Yes, Butch, a six-foot-six, 350-pound man who ate a full pack of hot dogs most nights. He decided he should say something about my weight but in a way that almost sounded nice? Talk about the pot calling the kettle black, er, in this case, fat.

Isn't family the best?

The Newlywed Gain

In Butch's defense, early in my marriage, I put on a lot of weight. Probably thirty to forty pounds over the span of a couple of years. There were lots of factors. In part it was just growing up and not having to make weight for wrestling anymore. In part it was because I lived with Melissa now and we had this weird habit called "regular meals."

But mostly it was because I was working at Starbucks and Outback Steakhouse, so I had a steady diet of white chocolate mochas and cheese fries. I suspect I gained thirty to forty pounds and lost three to four years of my life. Yes, this is my patented life span formula: one less year of life for every ten pounds of stuffing my face until I fall asleep. *Trust the science.*

Finding rhythms early in our marriage was hard. We were both in school, both had jobs, and both had separate internships in jobs we thought we wanted to have.

This is why Melissa and I did the unthinkable during quarantine and became a running couple. We were stuck at home and had nothing better to do. And I still regret it. There's just no way to get excited about receiving matching running shoes for Christmas. Honestly, I'd rather have had COVID-19. And we still gained weight! How could we not? We're sitting at home, staring at our food. If there's anything Melissa and I have learned about each other, it's that during a global crisis, we both tend to eat our feelings. (I also learned that our feelings taste like cheese bagels.)

MELISSA'S POV

COVID-19 quarantine was so challenging. Dustin and I hadn't worked out too much together previously. But attempting to do virtual school with three kids (some with learning challenges), run a struggling company, keep Grandpa Don healthy (he's in that vulnerable health group), navigate political and social unrest with a public social media platform—well, afternoon runs saved us. Sprinting the secret stairs of our neighborhood and huffing and puffing (yes, we'd walk too) helped us navigate our thoughts and feelings and release some of the stress. Everything was uncontrollable and constantly changing—the news, the guidelines, the statistics, the stakes, the gyms—but if we could steal twenty minutes to run together, well, we might just make it through another Groundhog Day.

- - - - - - - -

Thankfully (miraculously?), having come out of quarantine, we are in a season of health. I even lost twenty pounds. Melissa, as always, maintained a level of health and beauty that make people wonder why she settled for me. I don't say this to get points, by the way, because she knows it's true. And it's no secret that Melissa is significantly out of my league. So much so that when people see us together they're confused, and then they conclude, "Oh, he must be funny."

What's my trick for losing weight? Eating better food and eating less of it. Shocking health secret, I know. But don't think for a second that I've enjoyed it, because I've always had this theory that we have a choice in life: eat healthy or be happy. I'll never be convinced that food is not attached to our happiness. And now that I've enjoyed the benefits of losing weight through healthy eating, I know my theory is 100 percent true: I am healthier and less happy because unhealthy food makes me *so* happy.

Truly, there are foods attached to my joy. And I've noticed I tend to turn to them in the times I need them most. For example, when the Nickersons moved from Seattle to San Diego, we had everything packed up a week in advance in our POD. Literally everything, including the bed—we were sleeping on an air mattress in the living room. After spending the entire night feeling every single movement the other person made and resisting the temptation to "accidentally" put the sharpest part of our elbow in the other person's back, let's just say we woke up feeling like the air mattress: deflated.

Where did I find happiness in a time like this? Häagen-Dazs ice cream bars. Melissa and I had one every night for two weeks and we had never been more thrilled. There's a reason *fat* and *happy* go together. Santa Claus knows. He eats the cookies.

Speaking of cookies, cookies make me so happy I eat them till I'm sad. I don't stop when I'm full. I stop when I'm depressed. And I live like this for the entire month of December. I officially come home from the road around the first week of the month, and my first order of business is to go to the grocery store and transform our home into a dessert shop.

But then I control myself as soon as the holidays are over because that's an exception, right? Well, it would be except Girl Scout cookie season is two months later. You know, that time of year that brings little pint-sized drug dealers to the outside of grocery stores, and they put pyramids of cookie boxes on tables for me to buy.

What's wild is that people act like there are more than two types of Girl Scout cookies. There most certainly are not. I mean, technically, yes, but only in the way that a parent says, "Technically we don't have a favorite kid."

Samoas and Thin Mints—these are the only two that matter. Tagalongs? Trefoils? Do-si-dos? Gimme a break. Do-si-dos being your favorite Girl Scout cookie is like Arizona being your favorite state.

My favorite type is a homemade hybrid called Thick Mints, which is a whole sleeve of Thin Mints. I'm good for two Thick

We're Both Fat, but Only One of Us Is Pregnant

Mints in a sitting, which is a whole box of Girl Scout cookies. Like I said, strikeouts and home runs. And that's why diets never work for me. Not just because I can't eat in moderation but also because people who talk about their diet aren't moderate either. They're relentless in their pitch, the oversell, the hype. It's an extreme, and Melissa and I don't do extremes.

What eating better looks like for me is quite simple: oatmeal. God, I love oatmeal. Or perhaps I need to reverse the deity I'm addressing. "Oatmeal, I love God." When I go to bed, I legit look forward to it in the morning. Cinnamon, chopped-up apples for a little crunch. It makes me so happy that I flipped out on a Panera employee who wouldn't serve me any.

Panera oatmeal is a road comfort, which is one of the most important things a comedian has. My road buddy, Taylor Tomlinson, got me a $100 gift card to Panera and I got emotional. It's not the food we like. It's the attachment to reality. It was like the totems in *Inception*. I eat oatmeal so I know this is real and I'm alive and not spiraling into nonexistence.

But on this day they told me they wouldn't serve it because it was after noon. *Gimme a break. Really? This is not a big ask. I just want oatmeal. Did the guy who knows how to use the hot water tap go home? Tell you what: I changed my order. I'll take a hot tea, hold the tea, add oats. Can we do that?*

Oatmeal was part of my "this = good, this = bad" education.

Oatmeal = good, granola = bad (this kills me as a Seattle kid). One serving of tacos is fine, but don't go back and have seconds by using the tortilla chips to make nachos. Salad = good, but bacon bits and a full cup of dressing defeats the purpose. Muffins are just breakfast desserts. Disregard everything you were taught in the food pyramid as a kid; that's a death sentence now.

HOW TO BE MARRIED (TO MELISSA)

Moderate, reasonable, dare I say *average* advice is what helped me. No extremes. No pity statements.

Advice: Abs are made in the kitchen.
Me: Well, so are waffles. This doesn't help me.
Advice: You and your kids should go vegan.
Me: Well, your kid is over at my house, begging for a
    dinosaur-shaped chicken nugget.

The best test I give myself I actually learned from my kids, and I call it the "banana hungry test." Next time your kids say they're hungry, offer them a banana. Then you'll find out if they're actually hungry. Same goes for me. If I'm willing to choke down that flavorless, chalky banana, then I'm actually hungry.

We all know what dieting truly is. It's asking ourselves that question with every meal, snack, dessert, decision: *Am I going to eat healthy? Or am I going to be happy?*

That's it. Bad food makes us happy (at least for a second). That's why we do it. Eating better has also helped me because as a nearly forty-year-old man, injuries don't happen; they're just kind of always there. They're more like gophers that constantly damage your yard and every once in a while peek their heads out. They aren't going anywhere either.

Eating healthy is choosing to make your heart a little happier and your taste buds a little sadder. Not all healthy food is bad, but there isn't a quinoa dish on the planet that can compete with a Dairy Queen Blizzard. I will choose the Blizzard every time. Because knowing what foods are healthy and making choices to eat that food are two very different things.

Mel-atonin

It's the same mindset I have with sleep. I know how to go to sleep effectively. I do. Turn off my phone, limit evening caffeine, and read a book. Period. If I read, I sleep. But you know what? Reading a book isn't as fun as the internet. Heck, writing a book isn't as fun as the internet. Want proof? I just took a ten-minute TikTok break between those sentences.

I know that truth. I know how to sleep better. But self-control and moderation don't come naturally for me. I also have a challenging relationship with sleep. My body and brain cannot agree on bedtime. I am so exhausted that I can barely stand, and that's when the dialogue between brain and body begins:

Body: We should go to sleep.
Brain: Totally.

(Then we hit the pillow . . .)

Brain: Oh hey, real quick before you nod off. Here's a reminder
    of every single thing in your life that you're worried about.
Body: Come on, Brain. It's 1:00 a.m., we're exhausted, and
    there's nothing we can do about any of that.
Brain: That's right. I'm sorry. You know what? Instead, here's
    some bad memories, a scene from the scariest movie you've
    ever seen, and a reminder that you have to go pee again
    (you don't actually have to go pee—it just feels like it).

Side note: Why was this not on the warning label of aging? Peeing gets more challenging? *Peeing.* The basic human function I need to have because my body requires liquid. So I'm supposed to drink a ton of water but tell my doctor immediately if I'm going to the bathroom too many times? But I'm also supposed to limit my liquid intake before bed so I don't have to go in the middle of the night? Apparently I'm potty training again.

And I'm competing with two other generations of men who need access to a bathroom for three different phases of urine strength. We're like the three little bears but instead of porridge being too hot or cold, it's our prostates being too strong or too shriveled.

My son is a reminder of what I once was and my dad a warning of what's to come. My son is like going eighty miles per hour on the freeway, I'm slightly congested but still moving along, and my dad is like stop-and-go traffic. Poor guy, his pee has a stutter. Melissa, of course, pees great. (Small house. I can hear.) She's so lovely even her pee sounds like a flowing brook. She's just naturally harmonious.

And maybe that's why she requires music during mealtimes. Because she likes the mood and ambiance it creates and how it adds to the setting.

Nah. She just hates hearing all of us chew. (That's true love right there. Being with someone who can stand hearing you eat.) I like to hear the chew and sounds of everyone eating. Makes me feel like I'm providing for my family. Ahh, the sound of sustenance that my dumb jokes provided!

Melissa does prefer harmony—even on her plate, which looks a lot like a middle school dance: no touching. The salad can't touch the chicken, the chicken can't touch the rice, and so on. You'd think her foods hated one another. They refuse to associate. Melissa's food is so far apart on the plate their smells don't even overlap. She's moderate. Disciplined. Controlled.

On my plate there's a love fest we haven't seen since Woodstock.

It's not dinner; it's an orgy and celebration of togetherness. One plate, one food. None of us is as strong as all of us.

The contrasts continue with how we eat. Melissa chews her food. I attack my food. One time we ordered a Pizookie at BJ's, and Melissa cried laughing as she watched my dad and me scrape the plate like two bears cleaning out a garbage can. You'd think we'd never eaten before. (In reality, we were full and just go all in when there's food around.)

My kids are following my footsteps in this regard too. Melissa made a Pizookie for my birthday (I love this woman), and the kids and I attacked the family Pizookie with an intensity that was borderline alarming. Again, you would think we were malnourished. But if we've made anything clear in this chapter, it's that I am plenty nourished.

Activity Time!

See how well you know your partner. If your significant other could make any unhealthy food magically good for you, what would it be?

For me, it would be granola. For Melissa, chocolate. Just all things chocolate. She's lovely and artistic and all, but when it comes to red wine and chocolate, she is as basic a middle-aged woman as it gets.

For the record, Melissa has also put on weight during our marriage. She's had three kids and, like all of us, has gotten older. It happens. But all her weight goes to her butt, not her stomach, and she also took up being a group exercise teacher. So Melissa managed to gain weight and get hotter. Truly, she is favored by the Lord (and frankly, so am I, because her butt makes me break out in praise).

I don't want to make it seem like Melissa doesn't have to work out to remain in good shape. She absolutely does. But she'll be the first to tell you that genetics are genetics, and she's got good ones. Because this woman has a sweet tooth that rivals any of our children. And I share her love of sugar.

When I first started in comedy, I was often getting paid in dessert. I would roll into the driveway around midnight after doing two shows, and Melissa would wake up, eat some chocolate cake, and go back to sleep. Health gurus say we're not supposed to eat near bedtime. Melissa was straight-up eating-in-bedtime, and she'd still keep her womanly physique.

That's a struggle for me at times.

My family is all about comparison, and she's the one I can compare myself to the most. She has never judged me, but that won't stop me from judging myself. One spouse being in better shape than the other can be an enormous source of shame and embarrassment. Neither of which, unfortunately, will lead to change.

Real health changes for me won't happen by comparing myself to Melissa, though it helps to have encouragement from her along the way. It's not up to her, it's not because of her, and it's not her responsibility. But sure, some "you're doing greats" along the way don't hurt. Because if I want to really analyze what's behind my battle to be healthy, it's an internal struggle with self-worth. Like most husbands, I want my wife to not just accept me but be attracted to me. To desire me, to put worth on me. Catching a pattern here?

I once asked Melissa if she was attracted to one of our friends.

That went poorly. But not in the way I anticipated. She told me she wasn't attracted to him because "I am not really attracted to people based on the way they look."

This destroyed me on a molecular level. Cut me to the core. I would prefer that she had fantasized about him every day instead of hitting me with the ol' "I love you despite how you look."

Why couldn't I take this as a compliment though? Once you unravel it, it certainly is one. Melissa loves me for me and is attracted to my character and adores my personality, which is far more valuable than defined muscles and fleeting looks. Of course I could have taken it as a compliment. And of course I didn't.

I have managed to lose weight. I know some of you are looking at the cover photo right now, looking back at me, and thinking, *This is the improved version?* Yup. I work a lot—*ta-da!*

I am very average. I know that. I'm in the middle. I am fine. I am the Toyota Corolla of men. I am a very reliable product. Toyota Corolla is, after all, the most-sold car in America, and most people can't remember the last time they saw one. *That's* average. Some of you reading aren't sure if you own a Toyota Corolla. You're not embarrassed by this car; you're not proud of it. It's just forgettable. This is me.

The sooner I come to grips with this, the better. In part, this level of acceptance comes with age because health becomes much harder the older I get. I've had to change my goals. People in their twenties say things like "I wanna look hot naked," and in their thirties it switches to "I wanna look pretty good dressed." (As a side note, I'm convinced this is why Melissa and I became better dressers in our thirties. Yes, we had more money, but we also realized things were getting a lot looser and saggier and it might be best to dress these sacks of potatoes.)

It's usually when picking out clothes that we all have some sort of wake-up call around age thirty. You think you need a new outfit. Then you hit the dressing room, which has all the same lighting and mirrors of a police interrogation room. You realize, *Oh, this was not a shirt issue. This is a body issue.*

Perhaps Melissa is onto something about having manageable expectations. A lot of our pursuit of health depends on being realistic. For example, I'm not trying to get in good shape. I'm trying to get in a shape you don't notice. A shape nobody comments on. A shape you would never use to describe me.

"Is Dustin in bad shape?"

"No."

"Is he in good shape?"

"Ohhh no."

I'm in a human shape.

A Change of Heart and Pant Size

My wake-up call to lose weight was an innocent Monday in October 2020. We were planning Halloween costumes and I told the kids I was going to be Chris Pratt's character from *Guardians of the Galaxy.*

The table went quiet. After about ten seconds Gloria whispered, "Dad, no offense, but I don't think you could pull off Star-Lord."

Ouch. Mel had just said she was going to be Gamora, a badass green assassin. The few clothes she does wear are exceedingly tight, and there were no objections. But they were embarrassed at the thought of me in a leather jacket.

To quote Star-Lord himself, "Wow. This is a real wake-up call for me. Okay, I'm gonna get a Bowflex. I'm gonna commit. I'm gonna get some dumbbells." I didn't get a Bowflex but I did get a kettlebell.

Believe it or not, I was once an athlete. My friends now call me things like "deceptively athletic," which is code for, "We thought this guy was gonna be terrible based on how he looks." This happens the most when I play basketball. I didn't play basketball growing up, but I play a lot as an adult. It started when I worked at the rec center, selling memberships. That job might sound like a bad fit for me, but I was perfect for it. If you walked into a high-end, fancy gym, I agree—I'm not the guy people want pitching them on the gym membership. They'd look at me and think, *Well, no way this gym is gonna work for me if that's the guy who works here.*

But rec center fitness energy is a whole other vibe. The entire community goes to the rec center. Diapers to diapers. And when I worked there, people would walk in and be greeted by me, the perfect mash-up of Homer Simpson and Ned Flanders. They'd look at me and see something attainable. You know those before-and-after weight-loss photos? I always look like I'm somewhere in between the two pictures.

But then they would go to the Body Pump class Melissa taught and realize some bodies made them feel bad about themselves after all.

When Melissa was recruited by our fitness manager to teach an exercise class, she was just a member. She had no prior experience. That means she impressed the manager so much with her exercise ability that the person in charge said to her, "You should teach other people how to do that." It's like trying on clothes and getting picked to be a model. She's in such good shape that people ask her questions and advice and let her talk about her workout regimen.

Melissa's class was essentially an hour of squats. I celebrated this class because having your wife be paid to make her butt bigger is a real gift. Plus, she was making other ladies' butts bigger in the community. Talk about a ministry.

But I couldn't attend her class. Turns out watching your wife squat, bend over, stretch, sweat, and yell orders at you to do the same is not the easiest environment to focus in.

I was looking for tips and asked a personal trainer friend of mine what he recommended. His response was, "You know, for a guy like you, you can just do a lot of bodyweight exercises." When you think about it, telling someone to do bodyweight exercises is so insulting. "Listen, you're so out of shape, all you really have to do to get a workout is lift your arm."

I did try a bunch of online workouts, YouTube videos, and stuff like that. These were a problem because I don't trust people. I spent the whole time convincing myself there was no way that the exercises I was doing were what got that instructor to look like that. This was fake news. Best if I don't work out at all.

My goal is to get to a level of fitness where I tell someone that I swim laps and they don't assume that I've just started. I did start swimming when I worked at the rec center. I thought:

1. *Why not start taking my shirt off at my workplace and see if shame will motivate me?*
2. *This counts as a shower, right?*

I was a terrible lap swimmer. I can swim. Just not fast or in any way you'd want to keep watching. I am slow and ungraceful. Melissa, on the other hand, would swim during her pregnancies, which was hilarious because she would do the backstroke. So all you would see is this basketball floating down the pool. Then when she'd get her arms going, she looked like Baloo from *The Jungle Book*. But she, of course, stayed in excellent shape during pregnancy. Me on the other hand? Well, let's just say we were both getting bigger boobs.

One time I saw someone swimming at the same speed I was and felt good that I had a peer. I got out of the pool and realized she had only one leg. True story. She was the same speed as me and I had a literal leg up on her.

That ended my swimming exercises, and that was when I decided it was best to stick to basketball. At least I could score a bunch of points during the first game because the other team would put their worst defender on me. For that initial game I enjoyed a false hint of basketball with myself as a top scorer. A friend of mine named Jee, who played junior-college ball, said to me, "You would have been an All-American in 1964." It was the nicest thing anyone has ever said to me.

Workouts have come and gone, but changing the way I eat has been the only way I could really lose weight. To choose to be unhappy so that my blood still flows. My workout playlist is literally called "Workout music to help Dad not die young." I'm not happy about this fitness but I'll do it.

I started a program that really helped me pay attention to what I was eating. Helped me focus on food that had better caloric density and set realistic food and diet expectations. I mean, honestly, it just helped motivate me to not eat a mixing bowl of Golden Grahams before bed. That was the main thing. But also fruits and vegetables.

The diet stuff is important and it's why Melissa has always been in better shape than me. She is good at moderation. Not just saying it, like the Nickersons. Living it. That's not my natural way. If I see a pecan pie, I'm not eyeing the biggest piece; I'm eyeing the remaining pie. I go full O-Town. *I want it all, or nothing at all.*

Workouts take time and dieting doesn't, which is why dieting helped. It also helped because you can't get injured dieting, and injury was more of my early twenties than you'd think. Turns out being an aggressive in-liner, which had short-term negative social effects, had long-term negative physical effects. So I had three surgeries on my ankles and wrist in my early twenties, which meant I couldn't work out and had no good healthy diet habits. In other words, I was getting metal and fat put in me at the same time.

Those surgeries weren't on my back, but recently I threw my back out when I went to pick up my dad after his back surgery at the hospital. I pick him up from the hospital. We have to make one quick stop at the rec center to drop Claire off at art class. As I'm walking back, about twenty feet from the van—boom. It hits me. I know what's happened and I know I'm in trouble.

If you've ever thrown your back out, you know it's the worst. It doesn't ache; it's agony. A very sharp, intense pain. You can't move in any direction other than down.

So my dad is sitting in the passenger seat of our minivan, high as a kite and wondering why I'm lying on the ground outside my former workplace. Luckily nobody saw me or it would have been the most embarrassing thing to ever happen to me there since every time I took my shirt off.

I somehow get to the van, fueled mostly by fear someone will see me. I groan in pain nonstop for about ten minutes while my dad offers me his pain meds. This would be a terrible idea.

I consider it.

I finally get us home. I FaceTime Melissa to ask if someone

can pick Claire up. I then proceed to lie in place for the next three hours because when you're old, sometimes the answer to your injury is "just wait it out."

Later that night, the pain and the drama are subdued and I'm feeling better. I try to help get the kids down for bed because I hate to be a burden.

It happens again. This time in the middle of my daughter's room. Just like that I'm facedown in every mystery stain that rug has.

When you throw out your back, it's like you get shot but nobody sees anything. They just hear you make noises that would be humiliating if you were a dying baboon.

I go down. My kids mock me. The cherry on top is Claire jumping on my back.

If I could move, I would move out.

I look at Melissa, tears in my eyes.

"Please get me some ice . . .

. . . and a cheese bagel."

Chapter 9

The Baby Is Two Days Old. Is It Time to Schedule the Vasectomy?

Headaches. Poor sleep. Puking. Chills. Body aches. Midnight bathroom trips.

Who needs a hangover when you can have kids instead?

You know that "26.2" sticker marathoners put on their car to brag about how much fitter they are than you? Parents should get a "24 hours" one to remind the world that they are sacrificing their sanity for humanity's survival. Let's not forget that Lance Armstrong won seven Tour de France races, but he could only endure three kids. (It's unclear which task he needed illegal drugs to accomplish.)

Parents are all so hopeful and naive. You think you'll know how to handle each child. Then you have them and realize not only do you *not* know what to do; you don't even know what to feel. It's like children wake up and decide to create situations you could never predict or prepare for, just to mess with your head. Your little ideas and proposals are like the plates of dinner you serve them. At best they will tolerate them, but usually they just demand something else. Every parent has a plan, and then your toddler poops in the bathtub. What's the next move? Get the Shop-Vac?

Children take and take and take. And then once they've taken everything, that's when they really start to go to work on you. And the young ones are like leeches. They suck your time, money, energy, resources, dreams, will to live. *Suck, suck, suck.* And they give nothing back. Young kids are like having an employee who's robbing the cash register, but you can't legally fire them. And worse, if you yell at them, somehow *you're* the bad guy.

Please remember we were twenty-one when our first child was born. Melissa had her first child-induced breakdown the day *before* our firstborn, Joel, exited her birth canal. Me? I waited till the day after. (I've always liked to share things with people.) Like everything that happened that first year of being parents, the details of Melissa's tailspin are a bit fuzzy for me. All I clearly remember are her hysterics and our Hyundai Elantra. I've seen Melissa upset plenty of times. I've seen her at points of frustration where she's what I deem (in my head) "no longer on planet Earth."

But this was something else. It was an actual panic attack, a moment of Oh-dear-God-what-have-we-done-there-is-a-baby-coming-tomorrow-I-can't-control-my-breathing. It started out as a fight of sorts over only God knows what. Then, as Melissa elevated her tone and breathing and overall lack of control, I realized it was something more serious. I felt helpless. She was nine months pregnant and we had just bought our home. In hindsight, it was a miracle this only lasted thirty minutes and that with some breathing and a walk she was able to calm down.

During my first breakdown, however, I distinctly remember feeling like I had tapped into a heaviness and seriousness that I had never known before. I hadn't just bitten off more than I could chew; I was actively choking and needed the Heimlich. I've felt that every day since having kids. Like I said, I'm a sharer. I like to experience life's big moments with as many people as possible, so I greeted our newborn son with my own cocktail of anxiety and worry.

How to Have a Baby

First off, the experience is just gross. Not kind-of-sort-of gross. More like, the grossest thing you will ever see. The person you've deposited all your romantic funds into is yelling at you, pooping herself, and squeezing an alien out of a body part you've never seen in this form. Yet she's somehow more beautiful than ever. It's all very confusing.

My children were actually a pain in the butt before they were born. More specifically, a pain in the back because they were each sunny-side up. That super helpful, huge stomach you get when you're pregnant? Mostly useless to Melissa since our children did their kicking on her back. Even better? When they arched their heads out to leave the canal, all the pressure was hitting Melissa's lower back. It's called "back labor" and is as much fun as it sounds.

And then they make you hold the baby, which for some people is an overwhelming moment of joy. For me, it stopped at the overwhelming part. I couldn't believe that we were now in charge of making sure this human stayed alive. If you're a parent, you know exactly how crazy the whole experience is. Watching a human that you made with your own body be born and take its first breath is surreal. It's a feeling that's difficult to describe—something like happiness, but not exactly that. It's strange, new, other.

I'm sorry, but we make it far too easy to have a child. I had lost four cell phones in the previous eighteen months. But now I was legally in charge of the frailest, neediest possible version of a human—without even passing a test or getting a license. But parents don't think about this. They just have children because it's their favorite thing to do. Not *having* kids, mind you. *Making* kids. It's a cruel trap that God designed. If making babies were even slightly boring, the human race would have disappeared with the dinosaurs.

Eating brownies and ice cream is my second favorite thing to do. It used to be my favorite thing; then the other thing became a part of my life. But it is still firmly rooted in second place. Still, if every time I had brownies and ice cream there was a chance I would have a baby, I'd never be in the same room with brownies again. The cost would be too high. I would cut them out of my life entirely. I would seek rehab.

We would be better off as parents if there was a process involved. What if instead of sex, to have a baby you had to literally make the child. Like assemble it IKEA style. *You've decided to have a kid? Great! Here is the box of kid parts and a miniature Allen wrench.* If this were the route, there would be only two new Swedish kids a year, and one of them would wobble if you leaned on him. *Sorry about Johnny. If it gets on your nerves, just put a coaster under his leg.*

Don't get me wrong: I'm all for having kids. But I'm also all for *not* having them. Or at least making the process harder. Because under the current rules, it's harder to rent a U-Haul than to have a child.

I so vividly remember holding Joel and that first sense of weightiness, realizing that our lives had changed forever. It superseded any other emotions I had in that moment. Later I felt guilty that I wasn't happier. If it wasn't for the fact that I always feel guilty, that would have been a surprise. Instead, I just doubled down and felt guilty for feeling guilty.

And I felt anxious. We worried that the baby wouldn't sleep that night. Everyone slept but me. Even though the dad couch (essentially a two-by-four) didn't provide much comfort, it didn't matter. I could have been lying on a cloud made of puppy fur and wouldn't have gotten a wink of sleep.

My heart raced. My mind raced faster. *What have we gotten into? This changes everything. This is so much responsibility, and I can't bear it.* Thor *came out last week, and I didn't see it, so I probably never will. I guess I'll never see a movie again. Was this worth it?*

Activity Time!

How do you know if you're ready to have kids? Do you feel prepared?

No? Then you're not ready.

Yes? Then you're not ready.

Truth is, there's really no such thing as being ready. I'd say if you're at a place where you are willing and able to sacrificially live for something other than yourself, and most of your plants haven't died, then you're about as ready as you're gonna be.

Being a new parent is like the first week as a high school freshman. You're nervous; you're uncomfortable; you're constantly worried. Meanwhile, everyone around you seems so casual about it. How are they not freaking out all the time? Everything is scary when your kids are babies. They're so fragile. They don't even really look human.

I remember seeing the wrinkled face of my son when he was born and thinking he looked just like my dad. And not like a young version of my dad. He looked like the current old man that is my father. I couldn't be sure he didn't have the Benjamin Button disease.

It's amazing just how little you know and just how much there is to freak out about.

You are scared both that your baby won't sleep *and* that they will sleep too much. Yeah, that's a thing. The first time your child sleeps through the night, you'd think it would be a celebration. No, it's terrifying. You wake with a full-night's rest for the first time in months, realize your child slept through the night, and then sprint to their room 100 percent sure they're dead. And that's a legit fear! Babies are so fragile that they might die sleeping. How the Lord thought that's a finished product is beyond me.

Keeping Abreast

Making kids is the easy part. Birthing them is difficult, but one party takes on the majority of that stress. But raising children? Well, that's tough for everyone.

So much of those early years are tied into sleep, and it's the foundation of tension in a marriage. It's hard to be a good human when you're tired. I can't even send a good text when I'm a little sleepy. So asking someone to be a good spouse is like asking for the moon. You know, that moon you're looking at while you're awake in the middle of the night.

Because I'm at least 30 percent sure Melissa is gonna read this book, I should confess that she did most of the heavy lifting with middle-of-the-night baby stuff. I know there were rare occasions when I got up and actually helped, but that's how rare they were: we both remember them.

MELISSA'S POV

We were both half asleep during the baby years. Once we got through them, though, I've never slept harder. Now it takes several minutes for the kids to wake me up if they need me during the night. Maybe I'm just catching up on all that sleep I lost.

- - - - - - - -

Of course, there was a practical reason for this. Melissa had what those babies were looking for: boobs. I could rock them, sing to them, valiantly attempt to bottle-feed them. But at the end of the day, no father on earth can compete with a mother's boobs.

Boobs are a real point of contention between dad and the baby during this time. There's a lot of jealousy, as something that was once primarily used for your pleasure is now attached to their survival. It feels unfair.

Having young kids dramatically affects a couple's sex life. I'm sorry—I mean it *completely eradicates it*. I love my wife and have been sexually attracted to this woman for twenty years. But gents, it's a bit of a selfish move to look at your wife, who just grew a human from scratch and now is keeping it alive, and have the audacity to ask her to help meet your "needs." Just know that once that baby comes out, there's gonna be a season of sitting things out, and when *she* is ready to get back in the game, maybe you can get some playing time in. But in my experience, this has to be led by her. When she and the baby are ready to share the boobs, she'll let you know.

Hop In, Pop

As my kids aged and their problems got less breast-related, I became more useful. Trips to the bathroom, puking, nightmares—not only can I help those problems, there's a decent chance I'm already up dealing with them myself.

Joel was our first of two children who would have an allergy to staying in his bed. Joel and Gloria were, and still are, climbers. We have a tree in our backyard that is Gloria's refuge. She shares a room with Claire, and Claire can't climb the tree. So the only place Gloria can get away is up. The first time we realized this was going to be a problem started the way that so many problems do, with a *thud*.

There was no reason for a *thud* in our house other than a child falling out of the crib. It was the only logical explanation. We knew when we heard it. *Oh, dear God, our baby thought we were such bad parents he has taken his own life.* I honestly couldn't blame him. But no, Joel was happy. Just not in his crib. His slumber had ended; it was time to see the world. At eleven months old, Joel scaled his crib and had the confidence he was going to be able to do it, so he brought Elmo and Blue Blanket. Joel didn't just survive his thud at eleven months—when we reviewed the footage, he landed it.

Ah, remember the blanket days? Joel had Blue Blanket. Gloria had Beary, who "went to be with another family who needed him" (was forgotten at In-N-Out) and was replaced by Bunny, and Claire had Bank the Blank—who is still currently taken to school every day of second grade. Whoops.

Why does third-kid parenting feel so much like punting? These days our take on the blanket or stuffed-animal debate is to use it as long as it helps them. Because if it helps them, it helps you. They'll ditch it eventually. No adult has a blankey they need to carry around everywhere. And if they do, well, they have larger issues at hand. Besides, no adult can judge a child for that. An object that provides emotional support that you carry everywhere and is covered in disgusting germs? Not only do I have one of those, I give Verizon $150 a month for it.

Okay, kid climbing out of the crib. No big deal. This isn't super abnormal, right? A quick internet search and we realized this was so common they made a product for it: a domed net that went over the crib to keep the child in. Brilliant. It had a little zipper door so we could easily get them in and out. Problem solved.

It took Joel exactly two nights to figure out the zipper system. I'm thirty-seven, and I have problems with zippers at least once a week. Now we were in a battle trying to imprison our child in his crib. Our next move was to safety pin the two zippers together. So as it unzips, it immediately zips closed. This worked. *We did it! We outwitted our one-year-old. Game, set, mat . . .* Nope.

Joel made a hole in the net. To this day, we have no idea how. Like Andy in *The Shawshank Redemption*, Joel found a way to carve a hole into his dome prison and escape. Our baby Houdini won the day. He made it through, and before he did, he sent Blue Blanket and Elmo ahead of him. This is the equivalent of Babe Ruth calling his home run.

HOW TO BE MARRIED (TO MELISSA)

Once again, we had been defeated. That was, until we brought home the tent. The tent was a little toddler-sized canvas structure meant to be a traveling sleep aid for children that went on the floor. We used it for four years on two different children and it's the closest to camping we've ever done. Joel was never able to escape the tent. Instead he would just wake up and start walking around in it. We kept him close to us, often in our room. We all relaxed, and he started sleeping again.

Gloria, on the other hand, stayed in the crib a little longer but was never fooled by the net. She figured out the zipper with no safety pin the first night, and she managed to undo the safety-pinned zipper by night three. We got desperate and added a second safety pin (our most headlong act yet). It was just three nights until baby David Blaine undid both the safety pins, unzipped the net, and roamed free in the rat shack.

She performed even better than Joel. Though, in his defense, maybe she just had better motivation because his baby room had lush carpet, a proper changing table, a rocking chair. You know, a nursery. Meanwhile, she was in the tent on the floor of a converted carport with a space heater. She was motivated to escape, which meant we needed to get motivated to sleep train (which is such a funny concept, *sleep training*). *Not a complete product, Lord. How do I return it?*

Bottom line: marriage is hard enough; now insert children. Young children who demand everything from you. According to research, new parents (especially moms) are less satisfied in their marriage than their childless peers.[1] This makes sense because the marriage falls down the priority depth chart. And without effort, it can remain like that.

MELISSA'S POV

I'm glad you didn't pick up this book for A + B = C advice about child rearing . . . for feeding, wearing, sleep training, education, potty training, discipline, or technology advice. I know you will read all those books and listen to all those podcasts, and I say take it all with a grain of salt. No formula works perfectly. Every kid is unique and different at every stage. Try your best, and forgive yourself for messing up or not knowing better (*see:* us bed training our baby climbers, Joel and Gloria). Also, don't fake it. We are all a mess. I've been that new parent at the park playdate whose toddler keeps having accidents. Am I the only one? How are you guys dealing with this? Wait—you're silent on this topic but your kid has a Pull-Up on! We're all fakes; why not be honest so another parent can say, "Yeah, me too"?

- - - - - - - -

Everyone's a Critic . . . But They Shouldn't Be

If you're a nonparent, I want to tell you that I envy your life more than you can possibly know. But I also want to encourage you to be nothing but supportive of your friends who do have kids. Don't ask questions. Don't tell them your weekend plans. And for goodness' sake, don't give them advice. Just stand there and be their Wailing Wall. Take their complaints and hold their downward-spiraling spirits as they lament Old Testament–style. Because if you do anything other than this, you may lose them forever. Parents have no tolerance, no room for anything extra. We are ready to snap at even the slightest hint of judgment.

The meanest thing you can do to anyone with children—the big faux pas, the cardinal sin, the unforgivable crime—is to even hint that they are a bad parent. There is serious shame in failing as a parent. Justified or not, that's the truth. There is no forgiveness for being a bad parent. Not even from your kids, sometimes. It's like Oscar Wilde says in *The Picture of Dorian Gray*: "Children begin by loving their parents; as they grow older they judge them; sometimes they forgive them."[2]

Of course, the instinct and desire to be a good parent is honorable. That's why it stings so much when someone close to you suggests that maybe you're not up to parenting par. The judgment of a friend can feel like getting hit by a train. Perhaps worst of all is the judgment of a grandparent. They want the best for their grandkids so they decide to get involved, say a few words, maybe make a few critical comments. And . . . *Jenga*! The whole tower falls.

I remember Melissa's dad once doing something that was seemingly innocent. He recommended a parenting book, probably one we'd already rejected, so no big deal, right? The problem was that he gave it to us after spending a weekend with our kids, so it felt a whole lot like judgment (spoiler alert: it was).

Somewhat recently my dad suggested in a not-so-subtle way that Joel's attitude problems in football were connected to me missing some of his games. Honestly, he maybe has a point. But if you're going to play judge about your kids' parenting skills, you better have *crushed* the parenting game yourself. Because what our parents don't realize is, yes, our parenting looks different. And that's intentional. That's our goal. We are doing it differently than our parents did *on purpose*.

But as much as that judgment from a parent can sting, nothing hurts more than it coming from your spouse. Melissa knows my biggest insecurity in parenting and I know hers. Mine is that I'm gone a lot. I know I miss stuff. I do my very best to make the most of the time I'm home, and so far the jury seems pretty happy with that job. But Melissa knows she can hit me with a "You're always gone; you're never here; I guess I'll be doing that by myself" and unravel me like a Fruit Roll-Up.

Her? It's a well-known fact around the house that Mom gets stressed, and when Mom gets stressed, Mom gets . . . shall we say, stern? Yes, stern is the nicest way I can say that. Or the meanest way I could say it. For example, "You know, maybe every once in a while, switch it up and not yell at all of us all day. That would be a nice treat. Just a little variety for all of us over here." Purely hypothetical thing I said last week.

This is a low blow and a cheap shot. It's important to avoid these types of things and stay focused on the real enemies: nonparents. A nonparent judging a parent is like when I get mad at the pilot for a little turbulence. Yeah sorry, bumpiness comes with the jobs of pilot and parent. You can enjoy the ride, or we'll happily show you the exit.

Dog "Parents"

Personally, I seem to have a lot of run-ins with dog parents. Not dog owners—that I don't have a problem with. But dog parents. You know, folks who compare themselves to parents because they own an animal, as if animals and children were even nearly comparable in any way whatsoever.

Having a dog and calling yourself a parent is like having a Hot

HOW TO BE MARRIED (TO MELISSA)

Wheels toy and calling yourself a car owner. Yes, technically it's accurate—but you're an imbecile for thinking those are the same.

I remember doing a show in Solana Beach with a dog owner. She brought her dog to the greenroom. Before the show, she was open-mouth kissing her dog. I was repulsed. I was grimacing and may have audibly gasped. That's when the showdown began.

Her: You have kids, right?

Me: Yes.

Her: Well, can your kids even do this?

Me: Sit on my lap and make out with me? Legally, no.

Her (*talking to the dog*)**:** Just ignore that big, bad man. He's nasty. But not you. What do you want for dinner tonight, honey boo? Chicken or fish? Chicken or fish?

(intensifies kissing of dog)

Her (*talking to me now*)**:** I believe that all animals should be treated equally, if not better, than people.

Me: Really? All animals? What about chicken and fish?

Her (very *upset*)**:** Ugh. You disgust me. Just know that your kids could never fill your heart in the way my dog does mine.

Me: Whatever. Maybe that's true, but you just need to know, your dog is going to die waaayyy before my kids. And you might have to kill it. So maybe get a whiteboard and pro/con this whole situation.

(end scene, end relationship)

People shame you for being a bad parent and sometimes just being a parent at all. Don't believe me? Bring a kid to REI. Their

144

judgment is firmer than the grip of a carabiner. But you get over it and get comfortable. You actually get so comfortable that you start talking about having more of them. That freshman-in-high-school analogy still works because, just like in school, you settle in pretty quickly.

You can get in the cycle of having kids. I've wondered why that is, and it's because kids are like cell phones. Every two years you'd love an upgrade. A new kid and a new phone are similar: there's a lot of buzz. Everyone is excited, they come over, they want to hold it, and the most important rule is *don't drop it*.

But after a while the excitement has passed, and now you have a two-year-old kid, which is a lot like a two-year-old phone. It's got a lot of smudges on it, it never responds to voice commands, and sometimes when you're really upset with it, you're thinking about dropping it on purpose.

Philosophy 101

I remember someone asking me once what our "parenting philosophy" was. I had two kids under four, so I honestly couldn't believe what I was hearing. My eyes were barely open and the bags under them looked like the dark side of the moon. We had four people in a one-bedroom-one-bathroom house with a converted carport. None of us had showered in at least five days. I'm pretty sure I was drinking more coffee than I should be able to have and still legally drive. Our philosophy could be summed up in one word: *survive*. That's it. Just get through each day still being alive. Every night was basically a version of the movie *The Purge*. If none of us dies, everybody wins. Bonus points if nobody kills someone.

But parenting not only tests your physical survival skills, it also strains your relational survival skills. How have I managed to remain married to Melissa, despite all the stresses and strains, mistakes and missteps, criticism and shame? The important thing for Melissa and me has always been to constantly prioritize *us*. And not simply us but us *over* the kids.

Our relationship with each other is more important than our relationship with our children. Period. Ours predates them and, Lord willing, will outlast the time they live with us. And you know what? I'd have it no other way. Being married is hard, but a spouse is easier than a kid. At least I have an idea of what to expect with Melissa. A kid? Not a clue. One of my favorite things about Melissa is that in the twenty years we've been together, she's never pooped in the bath. That's something none of my three kids can say.

Melissa's lack of willingness to poop in the tub is part of why it's easy to prioritize her over the kids. Which, of course, is good for them long term. It's wonderful for kids to have two loving parents they can count on to always be together, blah blah blah. Sure. But we don't do it for them. We do it for us.

To do this, sacrifices have to be made. The biggest one we ever made was missing Claire's first day of kindergarten. Why? It was our fifteenth anniversary and I was performing in New York City for the first time.

Done deal. Sorry, Claire. We'll be there for your kindergarten graduation. (Well, we'd planned on it anyway. COVID-19 meant kindergarten graduation happened in the same place everything happened that year—our living room.)

This may all sound harsh and mean from the outside. Sure, I get it. But prioritizing your spouse can mean spending time away from the kids. This reminds you why you're together, why you got together in the first place, and why you want to stay together. So many relationships end when the kids leave the house, and it makes sense. Couples lose sight of being a couple. They essentially become coworkers working on the same project. Then the project ends, and you remember that, at best, coworkers tolerate each other.

My commitment to Melissa over the kids was probably never more on display than years ago during a road trip. I was sick. This happens. It's why I do the driving usually. But I had already been a little sick, so I couldn't drive, and now I was normal sick plus motion sick. Double the fun.

It's vulnerable moments like this when you realize just how mean kids can be. As I'm puking, not only are my kids not being supportive, they're mocking me. They are doing impersonations of me puking, as I'm still actively puking.

"I'm Dad. *Barf. Baaaarrffff.* Haha! What a loser. Is he crying? Hahaha!"

I didn't know how to handle this situation, so I just went with pure instinct. In between hurls, with spit still dripping from my mouth and last night's dinner partially on my shirt, I turn and yell at them, "*Look at me and shut up! You need to remember that of everyone in this family, your mom is the only one that I picked!*"

Melissa blushed, they went silent, and I continued puking in peace.

Chapter 10

Kids Are Always at "the Hardest Age"

When Melissa and I first became parents, everyone started warning us about this thing called the terrible twos. Apparently, our friends cautioned, when a child hits twenty-four months, they magically transform into a spawn of hell. Melissa and I laughed about their warnings at first, but in the end, the joke was on us. We have now survived three rounds of the terrible twos, and please accept this as my sworn and legal testimony that they are truly, truly terrible.

On the other hand, I remain unconvinced the terrible twos are objectively worse than any of the other equally awful ages. Have you experienced the furious fours? What about the hateful eights or the mean tweens? Ever met a sassy six? Each one is terrible in its own way. Our children are now fifteen, twelve, and eight, and I'm still waiting for the easier years I was promised.

Having children is the single most significant change in a

marital dynamic. Overwhelmingly, having kids leads to stress and less satisfaction in couples.[1] They're also expensive, costing almost $250,000 from birth to age eighteen.[2] So statistically, children will increase your tension and decrease your savings. They will make you angry, tired, and irritable. They will decrease closeness with your spouse and pull you away from important hobbies and friendships you no longer have time or energy for.

So next time your parents are asking why you don't have kids yet, just rattle off that last paragraph.

Couple's Question!

Couples, if you have kids, ask yourselves honestly, "*Why* did we have kids?" (Not *how* did you have kids, you weirdos. Stay focused.) Did you have a conversation about it? Did it just seem like the next thing to do? Did you feel pressure from others? A desire to have a family? Too happy and wanted to ruin it? Try and guess the other person's reason before sharing your own.

The majority of negative reasons to have children are pragmatic. What stats don't easily account for is why people choose to have kids. In most cases, it's a longing. They're searching to build a family, to pass on values, a family name, and a legacy. They want a home full of love and a sense of meaningfulness. And yes, 100 percent of children provide that.

Perhaps my favorite part of being a parent is seeing sides of Melissa and myself that I didn't even know existed. Parenting is so demanding and so difficult that it unlocks traits and abilities that we hadn't needed before. So many situations arise when you have to dig deep. And in that digging, you sometimes find gold within (also crap, so much crap in there with the gold).

The A&E Channel

Our household has a lot of little catchphrases that everyone knows. There are wholesome ones that we say to feel like good, wholesome parents. For years we've been telling our kids that all we care about is A&E: "Attitude and Effort." We're less interested in outcomes—test grades, progress reports, and athletic awards—than in how hard they try and their attitude along the way. I've been teaching my kids about attitude and effort from the time they were toddlers. I originally created it for Melissa, but they heard it and it still counts. (Melissa was in labor, and in true Nickerson sarcasm, I said I felt the effort was strong, but the attitude was poor.)

Currently our fifteen-year-old son, Joel, has two modes: lethargic and cantankerous. These two have nothing in common except that neither mode involves doing what another person says—least of all a parent. A&E has always been a struggle with Joel, who is our most "successful" child in the classical, quantifiable, and neurotypical ways. He is athletic, gets good grades, is in the associated student body, has a lot of friends, and so on. Of the most common ways our society measures a child's success, those come easy for Joel.

Despite that, A&E is not easy for him because he was gifted the cocktail of Melissa's self-criticism and my self-loathing. This recipe makes a successful drink, but one that is hard to stomach. When he's not beating himself up, he's a rad kid. Dare I say, even cool. I mean, who plays football and also skateboards? Sometimes I look at him and think Melissa might have cheated on me. But even if he isn't mine, I'm honored to be a part of his life. He's so cool it is worth it.

No matter how many talks and speeches (lectures) are given, A&E just isn't sticking with Joel. We've tried for years, and we couldn't get through to him. That is, until his third day of high school football.

If you're not familiar, high school football is the same wherever you go. It's a culture that cannot be altered or infiltrated no matter if you live in Southern California or South Carolina. On football registration day, the first words out of Joel's head coach's mouth were, "The first thing you need to know, we love God here." It came as a bit of a shock to those who don't understand how closely linked faith and football are in America.

After Joel's third practice, we picked up a very sweaty kid and headed to get pizza for Melissa's birthday. I rolled down the windows to air Joel out a bit, and that's when it happened.

"Dad, did you talk to the coach?"

"No. Why?"

"Today he gave a speech about how the only thing that matters is 'attitude and effort.' I couldn't believe it."

So on day one the coach quoted God's book. On day three he's quoting from my book. It was Melissa's birthday, and somehow I was getting a gift. But I was also thinking, *I've been telling you this for years! And one coach says it and now it sticks?!*

Of all the clichés people tell you about family, "it takes a village" might be the truest one. I always thought that it meant you'll need help with the day-to-day stuff: people to watch your kids, give you a break, bring you a latte, and so on. And while those things are important, I'm realizing now that it's so much more about what the village provides to the child, not to the parent. It's about the advice the other villagers have and share with your kid. It carries an unfair amount of weight to the point that it's almost frustrating.

After the solid catchphrases, there's the middle-ground ones. Like when we tell the kids to do something and they don't do it. Or they talk back. Or they delay in any way whatsoever. This is when the trusty "I didn't ask you to do this; I told you" comes out. Not bad, not good. Let's call it a neutral, though if it helped with the ultimate, never-ending battle to teach our children how to be more grateful, I'd give it top billing.

I swear so many of our problems stem from a never-ending battle in the pursuit of our children's gratitude. Which is like playing Putt-Putt with Tiger Woods. It seems like you'd have a shot, but no, it's impossible.

I don't know how to mold grateful children, but I know the answer is not giving them more stuff. Our children seem to be at their most ungrateful when, ironically, things are the greatest for them.

The last time we went to Disneyland will probably be the last time we go to Disneyland. After a day of a near-perfect Disneyland experience—short lines, all the rides open, Grandpa and his wallet also open—we were walking back to the car. A then-five-year-old Gloria asked for a piece of gum. Since we didn't have any gum, we said no.

You would have thought God turned up gravity, with the speed she hit the ground. Yelling, crying, pounding the pavement, she told us, *as we were leaving Disneyland*, "You never give me anything I want!"

In her defense, I do like gum more than Disneyland. But this grappling with gratefulness has pulled out some of the more iconic phrases and idioms in our home.

One of my personal favorites emerges anytime our kids mention something they want. Not food or an activity or something necessary or within reason. More like we're all just sitting at dinner, we've just finished thanking God for the food and Mom for making it, and a child blurts out, "I want something else for dinner."

Complaining about Mom's food will trigger me the fastest, and the kids know it. My home didn't have dinners or moms, so my tolerance for this complaining is nonexistent. It's in moments like this that I usually say, "Oh fun! We're doing the name-something-you-want game! Everyone go around the table and, for no reason at all, just say something you want."

Whichever kid first said they wanted something is usually pretty mad right now, and I'm reveling in it. I find it puts into context their out-of-the-blue asking for something.

And to answer your question, yes, Melissa and I share what we want as well. Mine is always the same, and the kids hate it. It's the same thing I put on my Christmas list every year: grateful children.

There are, of course, other catch phrases I often repeat to my kids:

"I'm not available."
"Be a better roommate."
"Be a problem solver."

Pros and Cons of Going to Restaurants with Kids

When you're a parent, kids always love eating out. But is it worth it? Let's look at the pros and cons:

CONS

- It's expensive.
- The kids don't eat all their food.
- You don't relax and enjoy your meal.
- The waitress hates you and it's obvious.
- You spend half the meal telling the kids not to play with the sugar packets.
- When the kids get loud, you get nasty, judgmental glares from other people in the restaurant.
- There's a 100 percent chance at least one kid will spill a drink.
- The kids don't say thank you.
- Dad gets mad that they're ungrateful.
- Mom takes it personally how much more Dad likes the restaurant meal than the normal ones at home.
- You fight on the way there, on the way home, and, of course, during the meal itself.

PROS

- *No cooking. No cleanup.*
    Honestly, it's a toss-up.

Is This Thing On?

All these little nuggets of life wisdom you share . . . you always wonder, *Are they getting any of this? Do they hear it now and will they remember it later?* Because it often feels like I'm back in my early days of comedy when I was bombing at open mics. The crowd is less drunk but equally ill behaved.

But I think so much of parenting is about persistence, just knowing that maybe if the kids don't hear it this time, they will the next. That's why Melissa and I use a lot of these little catchphrases and slogans. We're like a company trying to remind the kids to fill out their TPS reports (change the cat litter).

One new one I've recently introduced is "Take the *L*," which is short for "Take the loss." I love this one because it encapsulates so much of life. "You didn't win this one? Take the *L*, move on." It applies to games and sports and every other aspect of life. Something didn't go the way you want? There's nothing you can do but learn from it and move on. "Take the *L*" might be my first tattoo.

Then there's the more extreme catchphrases. These are rare but just as memorable. For example, though it's only been said once, Melissa telling Gloria "I will end you" is as well-known as the other phrases. The 1 percent uncertainty of whether Melissa was exaggerating is what really cemented it in.

The one that I'm most guilty of that makes the kids the angriest comes out when they bring up irrelevant details or some trivial matter. One of these happened recently when it was time for me to take Joel's phone for the night.

Our kids start getting ready for bed at 8:30 p.m. on school nights. Melissa or I supervise Claire. And by supervise, I mean do everything, including lie in the bed with her until she falls asleep. Yes, this is babying. Yes, this is probably stunting her emotional development. No, I don't care, because she's seven and she's our last kid and when your youngest wants to snuggle, you do it while you can.

Plus, I'm ready for a little nap at that time anyways. It's always impressive when I even make it through the story time. As much as I like the stories of Frog and Toad, ends up they are an even better sleep aid. I don't need an Ambien; I just need the Cat and the Hat.

Joel and Gloria know they get to stay up a little later. A little phone time; then they read until we turn the lights out. Of course, retrieving the phones always goes super smoothly too. They always hand them over willingly, with total compliance and no complaining. How could phones ever create any hiccups?

Usually it's Gloria that we have a hard time with on the phone retrieval, but this night it was Joel. I walk in to tell him to give me his phone. The conversation starts with me asking for the phone and him saying the phrase that triggers me the second most: "One sec."

When I tell a child to do something and they tell me "one sec," I turn into a drill sergeant with a private who just forgot to call me "sir." I want this done now. I don't want a timeline of when you will complete this task. I want this done.

"Give me the phone now."

"One sec."

"You keep saying that like it means something to me. You are not Amazon; I'm not asking for an estimated time of delivery. Give me the phone now."

"Dad, Bobby is spamming me with a bunch of texts."

"You keep telling me these things like they matter to me. I don't ca—"

"I know . . . you don't care."

You know it's a good catchphrase when they finish it for you. And they always finish "I don't care" for me.

I know these may sound harsh and dismissive. But if you think they are bad, you should hear the ones I don't say. A lot of times people are surprised that I'm a clean comedian and don't curse onstage. I tell them it's because I'm a parent, and by the end of the day I'm all out of swear words. A lot of good parenting is more about what you manage to not say.

I've managed to not swear in front of my kids except for one time. This came after each of them swore in front of me at least twice and Melissa had sworn at me at least twice that morning. So pretty good, in my opinion.

I didn't even swear in front of my dad until I was, like, fifteen. It was when the Mariners blew a save against the Yankees. Turns out the Mariners would continue to be a source of a lot of my foul language for my lifetime.

Though they weren't the cause of my first slipup in front of my kids. Mine was probably the most uneventful of the virgin cusses. Not a fight. Not stress. Not some cataclysmic event. No, I opened the door to the trash under the sink, the trash tipped over, and about six napkins and a banana peel spilled on the floor. I exhaled a simple, "Damn it."

Gloria looked at me, patted me on the back. "It's okay, Dad. It's an easy cleanup."

A&E FTW.

You Wouldn't Like Us When We're Angry

Families show sides of themselves to one another that nobody else gets to see. This is often for the best and often for the worst. Trust me, there are parts of me I'm glad only Melissa has seen and many sides of Melissa that I'm glad I'm the only one who gets to see them.

One of the bigger challenges that Melissa and I face is managing the level of anger in our home. As we like to diplomatically say, "We are a very *passionate* family." *Passionate*, of course, is our code word for *angry*. We can be an angry home. I'm not proud of it. It's not good. We know it's an issue, and we know it's an issue for a lot of families. According to research, "1 in 5 adults have ended a relationship with someone because of 'how they behaved when they were angry,'" and 53 percent of couples "consider anger a major concern" in their relationships.[3]

Anger stems from different places for each of us. Melissa's family didn't process feelings, and my family drank them. Which means in our house everyone knows how everyone is feeling at all times. It's never a mystery. We cry, we laugh, we fight, we play—all at 100 percent. We always give full effort to our feelings.

The passion really comes out during family game times. There is not one of us who views winning as unimportant or takes a loss particularly well. Once the pending loss is in the air, we start to show off our various issues. Joel makes excuses; Gloria tries to cheat; Claire breaks down; Melissa questions the rules; I shut the game down entirely.

It's more fun than it sounds.

Melissa rarely joins us for the games and has many times said she had kids just to entertain me. She's not wrong; they are super helpful for this. I like games, I like playing, and I really like playing the games I made up.

MELISSA'S POV

Dustin is so good at playing with the kids. They've made up a million games, and he's logged thousands of hours with them on the trampoline. (We've gone through three or four.) Our neighbors often text me about how comical their dialogue is—one kid crying and one kid cheating and one kid who doesn't want to cooperate.

I try to play on the trampoline with the kids, but if I'm honest, I have a hard time not zoning out. So I lose count of who is winning and just let them win. Not very fun! I'm better at doing an art project or baking with the kids, or making sure their permission slips get signed and back in their backpacks. Dustin and I have different strengths.

– – – – – – – –

Melissa had to endure these for several years. The one she tolerated the most was the simple Kick Game, where I lie at the bottom of the bed, perpendicular to her, and she had to try and kick me off the bed while I hung on. I liked this because it was fun. She liked it because it was an excuse to kick me.

Our list of family games I've made up is actually pretty impressive.

- Roll Out
- Chicken Nugget

- Trash Bag Raccoon
- Soccer Assassin
- Superman Tag
- Trip Up
- Burger Trap
- Jump over Dad
- Bowling for Kids

I'm pretty sure when the Bible talks about training up a child, this is exactly what it's referring to. And if you're a parent reading this and feel inferior because you're not as good at making up games, take heart. All that was required to get this skill was a lonely childhood.

The kids love the games and so do I. Most of them happen on the trampoline, where my best and worst parenting happens, often seconds apart. We'll be having so much fun together and then I'll go too hard and suddenly someone's hurt. Win, lose, quit, or draw—the games are never over until at least one of us is crying.

For the most part, our spats with our kids are similar to Melissa's and mine. They are intense but tend to end quickly and peacefully. They are less of a war and more of a shoot-out at noon.

There's an old adage that "the culture comes from the top." In a home, that means culture comes from the parents. When things are going on with your family and your home that are upsetting, it's worth asking yourself, *Did I cultivate this culture?*

A Tiff, a Taff, A Tussle

This is with the exception of Gloria, who seemingly loves the long, drawn-out, super intense, super emotional fights. I swear sometimes they feel like they go on for days. The saying goes, "Don't go to bed angry." But Gloria prefers, "Don't go to bed until you're angry."

What's the opposite of a tiff? A taff? A tussle? Whatever the marathon version of an argument is, this is what we do with Gloria.

The majority of these tiffs start with an honesty problem. I guess if you have three kids, odds are one of them might be sneaky. *Sneaky* being the positive-spin word for "pathological liar." (Of course we would never say that term to her and there's no way she'll read this book, so she won't know I said it.)

In reality we work hard in our home to avoid labels. We work diligently in our language to not call Gloria a liar. We don't like the definitive nature of a label. She's not a liar; she lies sometimes. Joel's not a dramatic person; he's being dramatic. They aren't a-holes; they're acting like a-holes. We don't want our kids to think that's all we think about them, despite their best efforts to show us otherwise.

Now Gloria's twelve. She hopes she will grow out of her acne soon; we hope she grows out of lying. She's lost trust with us so many times and failed at almost every opportunity we've given her to come clean. We have no answers either. Remember the cheating-chapter advice? I have the same nonadvice for raising a teenage girl or dealing with a kid who lies. All I know is it takes a village to raise a child and when you have a teenage girl, you're the village idiot.

Melissa and I have had some faith struggles over the years, but nothing will make you crawl back to the Lord quite like a teenage girl. Especially one who literally kicks and screams. Even though she's an incredible athlete, with legs as strong as a mule, her screams hurt more than her kick.

Part of unlocking the mystery that is Gloria (G-Funk, as I call her) might be keeping her busy. She's a gymnast and now a kayaker and canoer. Yes, our family has embraced San Diego *that* much.

She's also quite good at canoeing, and one of the only effective threats we've had with her was threatening to take away her trip to nationals in Oklahoma City. I don't know which is dumber: our parenting technique of threatening to take away her one healthy outlet, or making kids leave San Diego to go canoeing in Oklahoma.

The lying I understand a bit, but meanness I didn't see coming. Gloria is a lot like me. She has two emotions: chill and angry. But my anger isn't usually mean, and hers is exclusively mean. When she blows up on Melissa, it's a sight to behold. It's crazy to watch someone be so mean to your wife, especially your own kid. This is the love of my life. We've been together twenty years. She's my high school sweetheart. I just step back and think, *Oh my gosh, I could never talk to her like that . . . and I've been tempted. Gloria is in trouble, but I'll let her finish her thought.*

A lot of her "sneaking" anecdotes we don't worry about because they are often harmless. A popular story in our house involves Gloria's one year of Girl Scouts, when her cookies sale plan ended up being her sneaking eight boxes of Samoas and another four of Thin Mints into her room. Yes, she hid twelve boxes of Girl Scout cookies in a room that had maybe three hiding spots. But where there's a will, there's a way. And if it's a will for Girl Scout cookies, it's the way, the truth, and the life.

This sneaking of cookies has not stopped, and frankly, I hardly fault her for it. Thankfully for us, the kids are getting older and better at telling on one another. This is extremely helpful for parents.

Recently the Bigs (Joel and Gloria) were having a throwdown and I walked into Joel's room. As a parent you walk into these crime scenes a lot and you're trying to put together the pieces. You're not just judge, jury, and executioner—you're also the detective who has to put together the clues of the case while two people are yelling at you that they are the victim.

There's a broken lamp, blood on the floor, and, of course, no witnesses. You're looking for motives and going on a hunch. This day was different though. They decided to do the work for me.

Gloria: Dad, just so you know, Joel has been cussing when he plays *Fortnite*.

Joel: Well, Dad, just so you know, Gloria has a whole thing of Chips Ahoy! in her underwear drawer. Snitch for a snitch.

Me: Thank you for the info. Go to your room and bring me the cookies.

Wait—We Have a *Third* Kid?

Melissa always said she wanted four kids. But I'm not sure Claire was even out yet before Melissa scheduled my vasectomy. You know this was important to her because for me to have a vasectomy that soon was essentially to add another baby into the home for a few days.

I was very nervous about this, as one could imagine. Melissa tried to comfort me and told me she had done some research (I'm sure that was quite the Google search). She told me they said it only hurts about as much as when you get kicked down there. I told her this didn't make me feel better, as I had never scheduled a kick down there and I have never needed a co-pay for one. But I survived, and Claire became our final child.

Life for the youngest child is so different. They are both more cared for *and* more neglected. With Claire, Melissa and I are doing the "all-or-nothing" parenting approach. This is common for the youngest children, and honestly, it's for the best. When you have your first child, you do all this stuff that seems important but really is unnecessary. You babyproof the whole house; you get the best car seat; you feed them regularly. Unnecessary.

Youngest kid? Totally different story. You'll look at your youngest kid something like "You'll find food; it's in the house. Your scavenger instincts will kick in and you'll track it down. And if you don't, maybe it wasn't meant to be."

Much like all of life, by that third kid, you're so jaded. You've just seen it all. You have dealt with so much figurative and literal crap that you're a seasoned vet who isn't surprised by anything.

You think you know stuff going in. It's adorable how prepared you feel. Then your kid drops their toothbrush in the toilet, picks it up with their hands, and continues to brush their teeth. I mean, what's the next move?

A blow like this hurts, in large part because sometimes the bathroom is your only relief (in every sense of the word). There's a thing in the Nickerson home affectionately referred to as a dad spa. What's a dad spa? It's everything, is what it is. Long shower, clip the nails, have a cup of coffee, and lie down in the shower and question every decision you've ever made in your life. *That's a dad spa.* Sometimes I treat myself to luxuries like shampoo *and* conditioner, maybe a nail clipping, high-end stuff. If I really treat myself, I splurge and get the upgrade.

These are the things you live for as a parent of young children. Or old children. Or grown children. Or honestly, no children, I'd imagine. Which is why it's particularly disrespectful and hateful when, in the middle of a dad spa, a kid interrupts.

Claire almost broke me one time with a dad spa interruption.

This was an important dad spa because it was during a quarantine. So in addition to all my normal life and dread, I was also now homeschool teacher and had the dread of the world maybe ending.

I wasn't seven minutes in before Claire joined me in the bathroom. But she didn't knock. She didn't say a word. I didn't even know she was in there. That is, until I smelled it. Yes, she ninja pooped in the middle of a dad spa. An unspeakable blow and defilement of all things holy. This is the first time I've spoken about it because it's taken years for me to process and heal.

It took me two years to take that *L*.

Parent / Uber Driver

As the kids get older, there is less of *that* kind of activity and more activities you just have to drive them to. All spread out at different locations in the city. Football, kayaking, gymnastics, theater, swim lessons, art class—all of them starting at the same time in different places. We just added two new ones. All-day wrestling tournaments! Out-of-state canoeing competitions!

I help a lot with taxi service when home, but I'm gone on Saturdays when almost all of them happen.

MELISSA'S POV

I approach a new soccer league as a time to create strategic alliances. Can the little siblings play together? Do you have an extra seat in your car? You're grabbing sandwiches? Can I Venmo you for my little athlete? All parents pitch in how and when they can. Ideally we are all willing to offer help and ask for some too.

- - - - - - - -

Remember that old riddle about the fox, the chicken, and the bag of seed? You had to transport each of them to the other side of the river, but it had to be in a specific order or the whole plan would fall apart and they'd eat each other? That's Melissa's life every Saturday morning. By Sunday night, the weekend has left her pretty weak. Shout-out and much applause to single parents.

Parenting is not for the faint of heart, and despite what our parents say, it has changed. *A lot.* Modern parenting is so much harder in so many ways.

For one, discipline has changed. Spanking isn't considered the universal one way to discipline kids, and even those who still spank are pretty weird about it. I remember reading a parenting book that said you should never discipline in anger. What? Am I supposed to discipline them in apathy?

The point was you're not supposed to hit your kids when you're mad, which I get, but I think that's the emotion that matches the action. You really wanna ruin a kid? Spank them with a smile on your face. Then get that kid Groupon for therapy while you're back there.

But the bigger change, of course, is the internet. You spend so much time and effort trying to protect them and keep them safe and secure online, but they're always one step ahead. Kids are like Jason Bourne and their parents are the idiots running through the airport when he's already in the plane.

The internet is a blessing in disguise, though, because it is the one thing we can take away that gets the kids' attention. If a child has the choice of turning the Wi-Fi off or a spanking, they'll go get the paddle for you.

I remember a friend telling us that they let their kids choose their own consequences. The parent leads with a lecture and teaching moment, but anytime the child wants to, they can raise their hand, opt out of the lecture, and take a spanking instead.

When I heard that, I immediately asked Melissa if I could get the same treatment. You know, spare the rod, spoil the husband, honey. I'm lucky I didn't get kicked in the rod.

Children will lead you to desperate measures though. Truly, the most effective thing we did for years was lie to our children. We made them think that there was a program they could get sent to if they were bad enough. This program was called BKIM, which stood for Bad Kids in Mexico. This was effective for so long during their young years. It sounded just true enough that it would terrify them. (Again, we were lying; we weren't liars.)

We would milk it too. We would see a bus of kids going by on the freeway and say they were on their way to BKIM. "That's what happens when you ask for Pokémon cards in Target."

When Joel was about nine, he was onto us, but I needed it to work for a little longer. He called me on it.

Joel: There's no way BKIM is real. That sounds so fake.
You're making it up.
Me: It's real. Just ask your brother.
Joel: I don't have a brother.
Me: Exactly.

The van was silent.
I took the *W*.

Chapter 11

Love the One(s) You're With

H ere's a joke:

What do you get when you mix OCD with ADHD?
A distractingly focused marriage.

If you're slow on the uptake, that joke is about me being married to Melissa. Except, truth be told, Melissa is the only one counting because, like I said, I have ADHD and start twitching before I hit the number seven. But Melissa's OCD is not like others' OCD. Because others have an actual, diagnosed mental illness, and OCD is just what we call her hypervigilance, ritualistic behavior, need for things to be organized, and persistent repetition.

What about me? I've never been formally diagnosed with ADHD. But it's never really been in question. I'm the poster child for it. I can function in the right settings, but I have the behaviors. Aggression, excitability, fidgeting, hyperactivity, impulsivity, irritability. But even more so, I resonate with the characteristic moods, which, according to Dr. Google, are anger, anxiety, boredom, excitement. Not only do I live with these four emotions but they're also the only four I know.

That and road melancholy when "Cat's in the Cradle" comes on the radio.

One of the secrets to being married to Melissa is knowing and naming our differences. These are probably most on display at the start and end of our days. Melissa has rituals for both. They aren't glamorous, but they are consistent. Unlike me, Melissa can sleep. She rarely has a dream she remembers, I rarely have one I can't. She falls asleep like a light switch turning off. But waking up is a different story.

Melissa sets her alarm a full hour before she has to get up. Alarm clocks do not jibe with her. I'm a light sleeper who gets up for early flights and is constantly filled with anxiety and paranoia. Translation: if I have an alarm, my brain usually wakes me up about five minutes before it goes off.

Screw you, brain.

So if I must get up, I can. Right away. No problem. But if I don't have to, *good luck*. I'm more of a lifeless bean bag than I am a sleeping man in the morning. I spend my nights dancing for drunks, then coming home fueled with adrenaline to lay my head down to relive the night before (and whatever other trauma might be floating around in my subconscious). The challenge to fall asleep is the reason for the challenge to wake up.

Melissa gets this and it's why, on the mornings I'm home, it's unofficially agreed upon that I'll sleep in later. Usually my living-room call time is about forty-five to sixty minutes after hers. I'll take a kid to school, but it's the youngest because she starts later and the school is across the street. Not exactly laying my life down.

But ninety minutes earlier, we're in the thick of it with Melissa's alarm. Come to think of it, one shouldn't even categorize Melissa's process of waking up as "an alarm going off." More like a series of cataclysmic events intended to awake her from heavy slumber.

Her phone starts yelling at her around 6:30 a.m. from across the room. It always wakes me up first. Again, I'm the light sleeper. When this happens, Joel's alarm starts buzzing from the next room. The next hour is full of alarms that everyone is ignoring. I elbow (usually gently) Melissa to let her know her alarm is going off; then I cover my head with my pillow because I need to tune out the banging gongs of the next sixty minutes.

Melissa then proceeds to go into a sleepy social-media haze where she alternates between going back to sleep and checking Instagram. With each snooze button it becomes a little more Insta, a little less sleepy. This bizarre mix of gender-reveal photos and unconsciousness is how she starts her day *every single day*.

Then she's off to the races. Melissa is high-achieving and expects that of all of us. She also knows this about herself and tries to keep it in mind. Since she can never live up to her own expectations, none of us have a chance. It's that consistency that makes her seem almost alien to me. Melissa doesn't know how to be unfocused. It's not in her makeup. She does not have the ability to not be on task.

Just as she possesses characteristics that grate on me, I also must account for the ways I uniquely drive her nuts. Self-awareness is critical in marriage. It's not just about understanding yourself. It's about understanding how your self affects your spouse.

For example, I don't know how *not* to be distracted. As you have definitely witnessed if you've made it eleven chapters into this book. I may be the first person in history who writes an eleven-chapter book without ever having read one. I actually like reading, but just a few pages into each chapter, my brain decides to find something shiny.

Even the Birds Are Angry in This House

Melissa and I have many personality differences and conflicts. She's more emotional; I'm more low-key. (Is that sexist of me or just true?) She tends to exaggerate things, and I tend to downplay them. (Okay, maybe I am sexist.) Melissa has always referred to me as "the family cruise director." Up for a good time, at the front of the group, helping the family have fun. If we extend the metaphor, Melissa is the cruise-ship captain. I plan the shuffleboard and run open mic night, but she is the one steering the ship. And thank God for it because somebody needs to manage this thing while me and the kids are starting a conga line on the Lido deck.

We fight differently, we eat differently, we parent differently— yet by embracing these differences, we've learned to live together beautifully (like 88 percent of the time).

Because we have learned to be honest about differences and proactive about managing them, they've ceased to be serious problems for us. Learning to navigate them has created space for us to fall more deeply in love because we learned to more deeply understand each other.

I think the first breakthrough we had on leaning into our differences was back when we still lived in the rat shack in Kirkland, Washington. For whatever reason, there's always been this unspoken thing that couples are supposed to chitchat at the end of the day. *The workday is over, the kids are asleep, so I guess we'll talk now?*

This has always been a challenge for Melissa and me because

I don't enjoy small talk. In fact, I loathe it. I can't emphasize this enough. I find small talk boring and meaningless and trite and something slightly less preferable to Chinese water torture. I would rather stare a stranger in the eyes and not say a word for an entire afternoon than talk to a friend about the weather or ask, "So, how was your day?" when I already know the answer. I am pounding my laptop keyboard right now as I type this; that's how worked up it makes me.

Melissa doesn't take this personally. She knows that my brain just isn't wired for it. I have a natural aversion to meaningless conversation. I get twitchy, fidgety. I can't focus; my skin crawls. It gives me physical and emotional distress.

This made having the ritual evening chat with Melissa a real challenge, especially because she thrives on conversation. It fuels her. Frankly, I think she's an oversharer. She wants to be heard and understood, which means if she sees a crack in the door, she won't just slip her foot in; she'll shove her full emotional trauma and distress in it. She would, of course, dispute this.

Our differences on conversation is probably why Melissa and I have had a hard time having a lot of couple friends.

MELISSA'S POV

Dustin knows how to read the room. It's one of the reasons he's a great comedian. His superpower is knowing how people are feeling and what they want him to say. He can make anyone feel comfortable, and people often share things they haven't told anyone else.

I am drawn to authenticity, so I sometimes overshare my issues as a way to draw other people out. I am still learning how to determine whether I'm talking with someone who appreciates that sort of emotional dump. It doesn't win friends (or influence people) if I blindside others with TMI.

- - - - - - - -

Person A: How was your time with the Nickersons?

Person B: Well, Melissa wouldn't stop talking about her deepest feelings and shortcomings, and Dustin wouldn't get off his phone. So I'd say, not great?

But here's the thing: I love Melissa. I find her endlessly interesting. Yes, she's gorgeous and a great mom and has a killer butt and is a wonderful person, but those things exist elsewhere. Melissa is the only woman who exists who doesn't bore me (sorry to all other females who may be reading this book).

Even still, those late-night chats are a challenge for me. I can't focus, even for Melissa. My heart knows I should sit and listen, but my brain can't pull it off. Which is less than ideal since talking is her favorite thing to do with me. And I need to pay attention to this if I want to do my favorite thing with her later.

So how did we navigate this? What is the solution to reconciling our brains that are more opposing than Paula Abdul and the cartoon cat in that music video? What marriage miracle must be pulled down from the heavens to single-handedly keep our marriage from plunging into certain doom?

Angry Birds. Yes, the iPhone game. *Angry Birds* saved and continues to save our marriage. One night, after getting the kids down in the rat shack, I was sitting on the couch, playing *Angry Birds* on my phone. The OG *Angry Birds*. This is back before the movies and the merch. It was just a man and his slingshot of birds against the pigs.

Normally, as a courtesy, when Melissa entered the room, I got off my phone so we could . . . chat. This time I didn't. And Melissa didn't ask me to. We just started talking. We debriefed our days. Even though I was also playing on my phone, I asked deeper and more insightful questions than normal. I shared heavy things I was wrestling with emotionally. I never made eye contact, and somehow I defeated twenty levels.

Something magically clicked that night for us. Melissa and I realized a fact about my brain. If I can do a mindless activity like play an effortless video game, I'm actually a pretty great conversationalist. I just need something to make me a little less fidgety and a partner who doesn't take it personally. Melissa didn't take it personally because she was getting more out of me and from me than usual. She loved the result, and we still do this most nights. The only thing that has changed is the game. (Again, ADHD. I need variety.)

MELISSA'S POV

A lot of couples enjoy eating out and trying new restaurants together. But Dustin's ADHD increases if we take too long to order or linger too long at the table after the food. He worries that the server hates us or someone in our group is not going to tip enough. He's distracted by the constant noise and people moving about, and I want "tuned in" Dustin, which I know I can get if he's playing a phone game or throwing a ball against a wall (he

does this during phone calls). So we've learned eating out is not a
primary way for us to connect as a couple.

- - - - - - - -

There's simple logic here. You know how you have your best
ideas in the shower? It's because your mind is occupied, but not on
a task that needs focus. Playing games on my phone is a free place
for my brain to focus and be thoughtful and creative. (That being
said, showering with Melissa ends up not the best time for me to
have a conversation with her. I mean, yes, I'm focused. I'm just not
super chatty. I make noises, but they aren't formed into words.)

Here's why this matters: we did something that we found works
for us. Nobody told us to do it, we didn't hear about in a marriage
conference, and we didn't read about it in a book (certainly not a
comedy book). We found something that clicked for Melissa and
Dustin's marriage. It doesn't have to work for anyone else's marriage. It works for ours.

We've told this to so many people and they are appalled every
time. Absolutely aghast and taken aback. They can't believe I would
be so blatantly rude to Melissa and play a stupid game while we
talk. They're pretty much ready to draft divorce papers for us.

One of the fatal mistakes you can make in your marriage is
comparing it to other marriages. Don't do that. People should be
shocked by the things that do and don't work for your marriage.
Because it's not theirs. It's not supposed to work for them. It was
never intended to.

The single most important thing Melissa and I have decided to
commit to in our marriage is finding those specific behaviors that
make sense for us. Melissa can't resolve a fight when she's hungry.

Get this girl a protein bar and let's get back to work. I can't have a small conversation without *Angry Birds*. Judge all you want. I'm not changing and Melissa doesn't want me to.

***

The *Angry Birds* shock is nothing compared to the shock when we tell someone that we don't share blankets. Melissa and I ditched this one-blanket scam pretty early in our marriage. For the life of me I don't understand why couples force themselves to do it. You wear different clothes, right? Why are you sharing blankets?

People think of sharing a blanket as some symbolism of romanticism and gesture of togetherness. They treat it like sharing a blanket ensures a healthy marriage.

Incorrect.

Sharing a blanket ensures two things:

1. One person will be cold.
2. Two people will smell farts.

How this creates an ideal sleeping environment for someone will never make sense to me. Keep your symbolism. We share a bank account. I feel like that's enough.

Uniquely Y'all

It's so important not to compare yourself to other couples. Truly. It doesn't help. Find the things you like and don't like and embrace that uniqueness. You're not trying to have a successful textbook marriage according to some ethereal standard. You're trying to make your marriage work with your partner. There's no textbook. If there was, well, I haven't read a textbook yet, so why start now?

Melissa and I have a ton of these things that other people are shocked to learn about us. Perhaps the biggest is our schedule with me working the road so much. They picture Melissa just weeping herself to sleep at night (as if at times me leaving isn't a welcomed subtraction from the house) and they can't understand it.

But again, that's the point. They're not supposed to understand. Melissa is and Melissa does. First because Melissa is an artist. She was a graphic designer for years, still makes art all the time, and currently teaches art to kids at the rec center and in schools.

So when it comes to artistic ambition and drive for an unconventional career choice, she gets it. Of course she doesn't like that I'm gone on the weekends, but she loves that our family is built around live entertainment and the arts. That's a dream. We both love that this is what we're modeling for our kids. The path of hard work in a dream career.

Also, she's very much into it. It's not just my dream of stand-up comedy. It's our small business, and she's the CFO. We run a business together. She does the books, the merch, the marketing. I just make the product and go sell it on the weekend.

It works for us. And the people who judge us? It was never supposed to work for them. I know that because I judge them for having such boring jobs. *Congrats on being home by 5:00 p.m.! Sorry you hate everything else about your life!*

There are many jobs that aren't structured to be nine to five, off on the weekends, and don't include both parents always being home by dinner. If anything, those jobs are rarer than ever. There've always been pilots and firefighters and professional athletes who spend long stretches away.

Those types of careers are only increasing. Lifestyle careers require long hours without additional pay; content creators are constantly traveling to different locations. Aid workers, consultants, skilled teachers—millions of people live similar lives. As I have told Melissa many times, the Delta lounge is never empty.

Again, Melissa and I are unified on this, which is the only reason it works. Our marriage is about celebrating each other's differences, not trying to be the exact same. We've been together so long and kind of have your classical love story (so far). Because of this, people ask for advice and I always take it as a compliment—but it never goes well.

I always tell people the same thing: If you really want to know who you're supposed to spend the rest of your life with, ignore everything positive about them. This doesn't help you. We all like the positive things about people—that's why they are called positives.

"She has a great sense of humor!"

"I love the way he dresses!"

"She makes a ton of money. I'll never have to work a day again!"

Great. That's literally great for everyone. Listing off the wonderful things about someone tells you nothing about compatibility. *Not. A. Thing.* If you really want to know, look at the most annoying thing about a person. The thing that drives everyone in their life crazy. The thing that their friends and family cannot stand. If you are designed so that you can tolerate that thing, then that person's your soul mate.

This should be the stuff on a dating app too. There shouldn't be a cute picture that says, "I like to kayak." No, it should be a close-up of your back hair and say that you're in debt and have a sleep apnea machine.

There are ways to tell early on. Small things. Ticks. Gestures. The pronunciation of certain words. For example, if you're in a relationship with someone who says "*ex*-spressso" and you don't want to murder them? Marry them right then and there. It's *espresso*. There is no *x* in that word. You are uncultured and illiterate.

That's how I know Melissa and I are for each other. We can stand each other's things.

Melissa can't say the word *salsa* correctly. She says "sal-za." Like, "May I have some chips and sal-za?" Feel that tension in your heart? You've read it twice and you hate her already. We live in San Diego, fifteen minutes from Mexico. This comes up *a lot*. But I can stand it, so I know she's for me.

Equally important, she can stand my things. Which makes me far worse to be married to. I know that. In some stereotypical, How to Be a Man 101 ways, I'm a big letdown. I'm not handy around the house. Not my house, not a house of cards, not the House of Representatives. None of them. Handsy? Sure. And though this is flattering to Melissa, it's not super helpful.

I can't fix anything. Nothing. I can reset the router, and that's about the most I bring to the table. Early in our marriage we learned this. Something would break, I would toil with it for about two hours, and Melissa would enter the room and ask, "Is it fixed?"

I would inevitably respond, "I mean, it's better. *Fixed* is an aggressive word. I wouldn't put my weight on it, is what I'm saying. I mean, yes, it's fixed *if* you're okay with the bed being decorative."

Luckily, Melissa is very handy around the house. I wouldn't mind her being a little more handsy, too, but I admit if she was, we would get little done. We didn't know Melissa could fix things but we should have. She's diligent. She's a learner. She's the daughter of an engineer. She likes straight lines, can read manuals, and has the ability to focus on something for more than fifteen seconds. It makes sense.

You'd think that I would have picked up some handyman skills considering my dad is super handy. He was a carpenter for ten years and used to be working on stuff in the garage all the time. But for him, the separation was the point. My dad didn't get a lot of time to himself, and I wasn't exactly excited to be in the garage—so I just didn't learn any of it. Neither of us are thrilled that I didn't pick up these skills, and as my sister pointed out once, "It's just one more reason why Melissa is Dad's favorite child."

This all came to a head once when we took the kids up to Big Bear Lake in California. It's the go-to area for snow play in SoCal, about two and a half hours outside of San Diego. On our way down the mountain, it started to snow and we had to put on chains. We were staying at a campground, and the guy there advised us and then helped me put them on our van. By that I mean he put them on while I did nothing and marveled at his sorcery—I've always loved magic tricks.

Now, before any of you judge me—snow chains are not easy to put on. They are just a loose chain that you're supposed to miraculously find a way to get around your tire. This technology has not evolved since they were first invented; I'm sure of it. When I bought them and took them out of the bag, that's when I realized this is just a loose chain. It looks like a weapon you'd pick up in the old video game *Double Dragon*. No magnets. No auto fit. No Iron Man technology. Just a loose chain that I, the kid who couldn't tie his shoes until second grade, had to get around a tire.

This put me in a precarious position for a winter vacation. I'd wanted no snow driving up the mountain because then I'd have to put on chains. Step one: check. The Lord delivered; there's no snow. But then I'm on the mountain for four days and wanted it to snow because snow is lovely and fresh snow is majestic. And alas, the Lord heard my cries once again and snow magic ensued for four days. We were all thrilled, but 4 percent of my brain was still worried more snow would come and I'd have to put the chains on again the day we leave.

Not only did it snow, it was the heaviest snow of the time we were there. The roads were covered. But we had no choice. We had to get down the mountain. The kids had school; I had work; Grandpa had a Rose Bowl to watch. The chains had to go on, even though I was an atheist now.

As mentioned, the groundskeeper at the campsite bailed me out and got the chains on, but this hardly made me feel better. Because I know in the not-so-distant future there's an inevitable moment when I have to take them off because in typical Southern California form, I will be in seventy-degree heat and dry roads in about thirty minutes.

But how hard could it be? Taking off the chain? Undo one hook and they'll slide right off. They'll practically melt off. Piece. Of. Cake.

After about forty-five minutes of lying on my back in the dirty snow while semis drove past me and my dad yelled at me what I was supposed to do, I was considering just rolling off the mountain. The whole process started with me reaching onto the tire, jiggling the chain, and my dad telling me there was "one thing you need to be sure *not* to do."

To this day I'm not sure what he was referring to. But I knew from his deep exhale that I did in fact do it.

He wasn't in good enough physical condition to get down there. I didn't have the mental capacity to do it. We were in a stalemate. I reached a moment where I was content to either just drive down the 15 with the chains slapping on the road, or hitchhike and join a different family with a real dad.

It was during this moment of emasculation and humiliation that my knightess in shining snow pants exited the minivan. Still brushing Goldfish off her pants as she opened the van, Melissa decided it was time she took a stab at it.

She had them off in three minutes.

I had never been more in love. My dad had never been more disgusted. It didn't matter. Either way we were all back in the van, drinking hot chocolate seconds later. The chains had been lifted in every sense of the expression.

This is what I mean by embracing who we are and not comparing. This isn't typical. I get it. But who cares? I do 100 percent of the driving because I get carsick, but if I have to parallel park I get out of the car and watch Melissa work her magic. The car gets parked. *Who cares?* If this is what it means that gender roles are a lie, I'm on board.

I work the road. We don't share a blanket. Melissa fixes things. Next thing I'm gonna tell you is Melissa and I don't even like holding hands. No, no, we *hate* holding hands. We don't like it, not even a little. Neither of us enjoy having sweaty palms together. Why is this weird? We do plenty of things with our hands to make the other person happy. Can we take this one thing off the list because we don't like it?

Let me explain why we don't like it. First, I have small hands. Like, tiny little raccoon hands. Hands so small it couldn't make me 100 percent hate Trump because we shared that in common.

Melissa's, on the other hand, are normal-sized. However, she has psoriasis—which means despite being thirty-seven, Melissa has the hands of an eighty-two-year-old woman.

Translation: neither of us like walking around feeling like I'm her grandbaby. That doesn't spark romantic chemistry for anyone involved in that equation.

Of course, these are small things to exemplify the bigger principle: love the one you're with. Melissa and I refuse to make each other into something we aren't. We don't want to be anything other than ourselves. Not like anybody else, and least of all like each other. The last thing I need is to be married to someone just like me. Then the chains would never get taken off.

We're emotionally divided too. Not in that we have different emotions—she has them and I'm mostly devoid of them. There's a Lumineers song ("Ophelia") that describes us as a couple: "I don't feel nothing at all/ And you can't feel nothing small."[1]

This is us to a T. If Melissa is gonna have an emotion, she's swinging for the fences and having a big one. This is tough for me because I hate drama, and feelings are *all* drama. Not Melissa. Our kids don't need drama class at school; they got a master class at home. Our home may be one of the few in history where our kids go to public middle school and high schools and there's less drama there than at home.

The real point of contention is that when an issue comes up, Melissa almost always exaggerates how bad it is and I always downplay how significant it is. Meaning the truth is always somewhere in between us. For example, if one of the kids has an F in math, Melissa goes to "She's gonna fail out of school, be living with us forever, and probably start selling and using meth." And I retort with "She'll figure it out."

The truth is she is having a hard time and will get through it, but she needs help and resources. Like I said, somewhere in the middle. The trick becomes for us to realize that and move forward.

Thinking about it, we have so many of those little things that, from the outside in, would drive people bonkers and cause them to worry about us. For example:

- I don't wear a wedding ring probably half the time. I take it off when I work out, shower, or sleep. It bothers me so I take it off. Add to that my forgetfulness, which means we've lost and reordered that $12.99 Amazon ring about fifty times.
- We don't like regular date nights. Just not a fan. Don't like spending the money. Don't like when couples act as if it's the key to their marriage. We like being sporadic and hate being basic. *No date night it is.*
- One year I got Melissa a vacuum for Valentine's Day. People were appalled. She loved it.
- I like holiday gifts to be surprises. Even if Melissa strikes out on her gift giving, I appreciate the thought. Melissa would prefer to pick out her own gifts.
- I like shopping with Melissa and for Melissa. Take that, stereotypes.
- When we watch TV together, we sit on separate couches.
- And you thought the blanket was bad? Even with our two separate blankets, *we never* cuddle in bed. We don't like it. We don't like the way it feels and we don't like what it stands for. (You know why young couples cuddle in bed? Because they're still afraid that person is gonna leave. They aren't cuddling; they're holding on. That's not romance. That's a hostage situation. They'd leave if they could.)

HOW TO BE MARRIED (TO MELISSA)

Melissa and I in our happiest, most content moments of marriage get in bed and wish the other person were farther away. We don't want to feel each other, let alone touch each other. It was the happy couple that invented the California king mattress because the king-sized mattress didn't suffice. *"Farther away!"*

Remember the Tempur-Pedic mattress commercial where the girl was jumping next to the glass of wine that didn't spill? That's agreeing with me. "You could be jumping next to me in the bed; I just don't want to know you're there. You've taken my daytime dreams; could I have these, please?"

It's this specification that makes me useless in giving dating advice.

A friend going through a breakup recently asked if Melissa was steady.

My response? Yes and no. She's steady, but my version of steady. Emotionally? Not at all. Diligent, thorough, filling in my gaps like glue in a crevice? One hundred percent. But if you're envisioning a sweet, dutiful, steady housewife, she ain't it. She's passionate and intense. She does nothing with less than 100 percent feeling and conviction. She'll rip your head off and then kiss the injury.

And best of all, she's mine.

Acknowledgments

Thank you to every couple who has helped our marriage including:

- Rhea and Geno Hunt
- Kevin and Lisa Mackey
- Micah and Lindsey Carioto
- Lee and Kristi Crum
- Mike and Val O'Neil
- Jessica and Tripp Forgeng

Thank you to my three amazingly unique and hilariously wonderful kids: Joel, Gloria, and Claire.

Thank you to the friends and family who helped during our hard financial years with childcare, money, opportunities, cheap labor, and love:

- All four of our parents and our extended families
- Sendhil Panchadsaram
- Cyndi Pedersen
- Jake and Lindsey Chambers

ACKNOWLEDGMENTS

- Maria Todaro
- Rick and Margaret Peacock
- Peter Delgado
- Tim Hawkins
- Zoltan Kaszas
- Our extended church and Kroc Center communities
- Mel's "Mom Support Group": Lora, Olivia, and Shay.

Thank you to Taylor Tomlinson for your friendship and the very kind and sweet foreword. It's nice to have you open for me for once.

Those who buy tickets to my shows, the *Don't Make Me Come Back There* podcast listeners (The Backseaters), my world-class Patreons, and the internet commenters who help the algorithms on YouTube, Instagram, Facebook, Twitter, and TikTok.

Thank you to T. M. Sell for teaching me how to write.

To my literary agent, Jonathan Merritt, for pushing me on this project and believing that you could make money off me.

Thank you to my editorial team. To my world-class editor Jenny Baumgartner, who I consider myself lucky to have as an editor and even luckier to know as a person. Truly, Jenny, you are a top-shelf human. Also to my entire HarperCollins team: Stephanie Tresner, Claire Drake, Sara Broun, and Brigitta Nortker. Thank you all for doing the heavy lifting in getting this book out. I quite literally couldn't have done it without you. Because I don't know how to.

Notes

Chapter 1: If You Like *Fight Club*, You'll Love Marriage

1. Brittany Wong, "We Asked Divorced People to Share the Fight That Ended Their Marriage," *Huffington Post*, August 3, 2018, updated January 4, 2021, https://www.huffpost.com/entry/divorced-fight-that-ended-marriage_n_5b633831e4b0de86f49f15c5.

Chapter 2: A Full Heart Won't Fill an Empty Bank Account

1. Elizabeth Cole, "Money Ruining Marriages in America: A Ramsey Solutions Study," Ramsey, February 6, 2018, https://www.ramseysolutions.com/company/newsroom/releases/money-ruining-marriages-in-america.

Chapter 4: Great Sexpectations

1. Mike Birbiglia, Spotify, track 7 "Sex, Tennis, and Pandas," *Two Drink Mike*, 2006.
2. Stephen Waldron, "Couples Who Have Sex Weekly Are Happiest," Society for Personality and Social Psychology, November 17, 2015, https://www.spsp.org/news-center/press-releases/sex-frequency-study.

Chapter 6: Marriage Is About Balance, but Sometimes It Gives You Vertigo

1. Lea Rose Emery, "7 Tips for Creating a Balanced Relationship with Your Partner," Bustle, April 25, 2018, https://www.bustle.com/p/how-to-create-a-balanced-relationship-with-your-partner-8882248.
2. Wendy Klein, Carolina Izquierdo, and Thomas N. Bradbury, "The Difference Between a Happy Marriage and Miserable One: Chores," *Atlantic*, March 1, 2013, https://www.theatlantic.com/sexes/archive/2013/03/the-difference-between-a-happy-marriage-and-miserable-one-chores/273615/.
3. Garson O'Toole, "Youth Is Wasted on the Young," Quote Investigator, last updated February 6, 2019, https://quoteinvestigator.com/2015/09/07/young/.

NOTES

Chapter 7: Our "Footprints in the Sand" Are on Different Beaches

1. Richard Asa, "Religion and Relationships: Changing the Tenor of Your Faith Can Take a Toll," *Chicago Tribune*, March 17, 2015, https://www.chicagotribune.com /lifestyles/sc-fam-0324-faith-changing-relationship-20150317-story.html.

Chapter 8: We're Both Fat, but Only One of Us Is Pregnant

1. Robert G. Wood, Brian Goesling, and Sarah Avellar, "The Effects of Marriage on Health: A Synthesis of Recent Research Evidence," Office of the Assistant Secretary for Planning and Evaluation, June 30, 2007, https://aspe.hhs.gov/reports /effects-marriage-health-synthesis-recent-research-evidence-research-brief.

Chapter 9: The Baby Is Two Days Old. Is It Time to Schedule the Vasectomy?

1. Sarah Szczypinksi, "The 'Happiness Gap': What Having Kids Really Does to Your Marriage," Today.com, June 27, 2017, https://www.today.com/parents/does -having-children-destroy-happy-marriage-t113028.
2. Oscar Wilde, *The Picture of Dorian Gray* (SDE Classics, 2019), 57.

Chapter 10: Kids Are Always at "the Hardest Age"

1. Elizabeth Scott, "Coping with the Stress Children Add to a Marriage," VeryWellMind, updated March 8, 2021, https://www.verywellmind.com /coping-with-stress-that-children-add-to-marriage-4121318.
2. Elyssa Kirkham, "A Breakdown of the Cost of Raising a Child," Plutus Foundation, February 2, 2021, https://plutusfoundation.org/2021/a-breakdown -of-the-cost-of-raising-a-child/.
3. Joseph Nolan, "How Anger Will Unravel Your Relationship," The Healthy Marriage, February 28, 2020, https://thehealthymarriage.org/how-anger-will -unravel-your-relationship/.

Chapter 11: Love the One(s) You're With

1. Lumineers, "Ophelia," by Wesley Schultz and Jeremy Fraitese, in *Cleopatra*, Dualtone Records, 2016, album.

About the Author

Dustin Nickerson is "the world's most average person." A comedian who performs in more than 300 shows a year, his videos have been viewed more than 20 million times and he has appeared on Comedy Central, Hulu, Fox, and Netflix alongside Kevin Hart. His stand-up comedy special, *Overwhelmed*, which was produced by KevOnStage, was one of the highest-rated comedy specials on Amazon Prime and has been viewed more than 130,000 times on YouTube. He has been married to his high school sweetheart, Melissa, for more than seventeen years, and together, they host the popular *Don't Make Me Come Back There* podcast in between raising their three children. They live in San Diego, California.